# ISSUES AND ALTERNATIVES

## IN

# EDUCATIONAL
# PHILOSOPHY

# ISSUES AND ALTERNATIVES

## IN

# EDUCATIONAL PHILOSOPHY

**Second Edition**

## George R. Knight

Andrews University Press
Berrien Springs, Michigan

Printing: 7 6 5                    Year: 95 94

"An education that fails to consider the fundamental questions of human existence—the questions about the meaning of life and the nature of truth, goodness, beauty, and justice, with which philosophy is concerned—is a very inadequate type of education."

—Harold Titus

"At present, opinion is divided about the subjects of education. People do not take the same view about what should be learned by the young, either with a view to human excellence or a view to the best possible life; nor is it clear whether education should be directed mainly to the intellect or to moral character . . .[,] whether the proper studies to be pursued are those that are useful in life, or those which make for excellence, or those that advance the bounds of knowledge. . . . Men do not all honor the same distinctive human excellence and so naturally they differ about the proper training for it."

—Aristotle

*To my students in educational philosophy; individuals whose probings extended and refined my thinking*

# PREFACE

*Issues and Alternatives in Educational Philosophy* is a survey of philosophies and philosophic issues that are relevant to the educational profession. It highlights the relationship between philosophic starting points and educational outcomes—between theory and practice. This short book makes no claim to comprehensive treatment of either educational or philosophical categories. It is a survey, and, as such, it does not seek to answer all the questions raised. On the contrary, many questions have been deliberately left unanswered or unexplained in the hope that such an approach might stimulate discussion and continuing thought about those questions. Thinking is an ongoing process, and one of the most beneficial results of the study of educational philosophy is obtained if students reach the place where they are unable to think of educational practices in isolation from the basic questions of life and meaning that give those practices significance.

This book has been developed with brevity, breadth of coverage, and clarity of presentation as goals. There is no lack of medium-sized and larger textbooks on educational philosophy available, but there is a dearth of short introductory texts. In addition, the existing brief treatments generally do not cover the full range of options. *Issues and Alternatives* has been developed to fill that gap. It is a brief survey text that is especially suited to fit the needs of undergraduate survey courses in educational philosophy, graduate students who need a quick review of the topic, and teachers of educational philosophy who want their students to spend maximum time in primary sources, while utilizing a wide-ranging survey text for orientation and overview.

*Issues and Alternatives* is divided into three sections. Part I deals with basic issues in philosophy and the relationship between philosophy and education. Part II is a survey of how traditional and modern philosophies have faced the basic philosophic issues, and the alternatives they have developed for educational practice. Part III discusses the need for developing a personal philosophy of education, some ways of building such a philosophy, and some of the challenges involved in implementing that philosophy.

The author is indebted to many people for his ideas. I would particularly like to express my gratitude to Joshua Weinstein for introducing me to the field of educational philosophy, and to my wife, Betty, who forced me to ask questions when I was already satisfied with the answers. The result of their influence on me has been growth and perseverance. Needless to say, I am also indebted to a host of writers, teachers, and speakers who have contributed to my education over the years. Many of the thoughts expressed in this volume have been gleaned from these sources. It should also be evident that originality is not a virtue (nor a goal) of a survey text—this is true of *Issues and Alternatives*.

George R. Knight
April 19, 1982

## A Note on the Second Edition

The reception of the first edition of *Issues and Alternatives in Educational Philosophy* far exceeded its author's expectations. Its numerous printings and wide use have validated the helpfulness of the general approach taken. This second edition, therefore, makes no major changes in either structure or content. The changes revolve around updating (especially in relation to conservative reactions to the liberal educational theories of the 1960s and 1970s), clarifying, enriching, and editing the rough spots.

May 22, 1989

# CONTENTS

ix

# ISSUES AND ALTERNATIVES IN EDUCATIONAL PHILOSOPHY

# THE NATURE OF PHILOSOPHY AND EDUCATION $\qquad$ 1

## Why Study Philosophy of Education?

**M**indlessness"[1] is the most pertinent and accurate criticism of American education in the twentieth century. There has been a great deal of activity in the field of educational innovation and experimentation, but most of it has not been adequately evaluated in terms of purpose, goals, and actual needs. Charles Silberman noted that education "has suffered too long from too many answers and too few questions."[2]

Neil Postman and Charles Weingartner have indicated that mindlessness in education is a natural outcome for a society which has traditionally been concerned with the "how" rather than the "why" of modern life. America has been making an unrelenting assault on technique for more than a century. As a nation, it has been busy creating new techniques for traveling, communicating, healing, cleaning, dying, and killing. The American people, however, have seldom asked whether or not they wanted the improvements, needed them, should have them, or whether they would come at too high a cost. The very word "progress" has come to be seen in terms of new methods. This

---

[1] Charles E. Silberman, *Crisis in the Classroom: The Remaking of American Education* (New York: Vintage Books, 1970), p. 11.

[2] Ibid., p. 470.

1

mentality, claim Postman and Weingartner, has been adopted by the educationalists of America who are busy creating new techniques for teaching spelling, new methods for teaching arithmetic to two-year-olds, new ways of keeping school halls quiet, and new modes for measuring intelligence. Educators have been so busy creating and implementing new methodology that they have often failed to ask such questions as whether two-year-old mathematicians are worth having.[3]

"Why all this education? To what purpose?"[4] These are two of the most important questions that must be faced. Yet they are generally not seriously confronted. Educators have been concerned more with motion than progress, with means than ends. They have failed to ask the larger question of purpose; and the professional training of educators, with its emphasis on methodology, has largely set them up for this problem.

Columbia University's Lawrence Cremin met the issue squarely when he noted that

> too few educational leaders in the United States are genuinely preoccupied with educational issues because they have no clear ideas about education. And if we look at the way these leaders have been recruited and trained, there is little that would lead us to expect otherwise. They have too often been managers, facilitators, politicians in the narrowest sense. They have been concerned with building buildings, balancing budgets, and pacifying parents, but they have not been prepared to spark a great public dialogue about the ends and means of education. And in the absence of such a dialogue, large segments of the public have had, at best, a limited understanding of the whys and wherefores of popular schooling.[5]

[3] Neil Postman and Charles Weingartner, *The School Book: For People Who Want to Know What All the Hollering Is About* (New York: Dell Publishing Co., 1973), pp. 295-97.

[4] Lawrence A. Cremin, *The Genius of American Education* (New York: Vintage Books, 1965), p. 30.

[5] Ibid., pp. 111-12.

There is a strong need for the preparation of a new breed of professional educators who are able to focus on "thought about purpose" and "to think about what they are doing and why they are doing it."[6] Certain educational thought leaders are calling for professional training that emphasizes studies in the humanities of education—those studies of the history, philosophy, and literature of education that will enable educators to develop a clear vision regarding the purpose of education and its relation to the meaning of life.

In the twentieth century, studies in the humanities of education have been neglected in the training of educational professionals because their immediate utility has been difficult to demonstrate. But, notes Cremin, "it is their ultimate utility that really matters."[7] After all, it is not even possible to talk in terms of the utility of educational means unless individuals know what they desire as an end product and why they desire one particular end product above other possible outcomes. When a desired goal is in mind, then a person is in a position to think in terms of the relative value of the various methodologies that will aid in reaching that destination.

The task of educational philosophy is to bring future teachers, principals, superintendents, counselors, and curriculum specialists into face-to-face contact with the large questions underlying the meaning and purpose of life and education. To understand these questions, the student must wrestle with such issues as the nature of reality, the meaning and source of knowledge, and the structure of values. Educational philosophy must bring students into a position from which they can intelligently evaluate alternative ends, relate their aims to desired ends, and select pedagogical methods that harmonize with their aims. Thus a major task of educational philosophy is to help educators think meaningfully about the total educational and life process, so that they will be in a better position to develop a consistent and

---

[6] Silberman, *Crisis in the Classroom,* p. 11.

[7] Cremin, *The Genius of American Education,* p. 112.

comprehensive program that will assist their students in arriving at the desired goal.

In summary, the study of educational philosophy is (1) to help educators become acquainted with the basic problems of education, (2) to enable them to evaluate better the wide variety of suggestions offered as solutions to these problems, (3) to assist in clarifying thinking about the goals of both life and education, and (4) to guide in the development of an internally consistent point of view and a program that relates realistically to the larger world context.

# What Is Philosophy?

Literally, the word "philosophy" means love of wisdom. It should be noted, however, that loving wisdom does not make one a philosopher. Philosophy, in its technical sense, might best be thought of in three aspects: an activity, a set of attitudes, and a body of content (see figure 1).[8]

## Philosophy as an Activity

The activity aspect of philosophy is best seen by noting what philosophers do. Synthesizing, speculating, prescribing, and analyzing are four activities that have traditionally been at the center of philosophic endeavors.

The synthesizing role of the philosopher rests on mankind's desire and need to possess a comprehensive and consistent view of life that provides a basis upon which to unify thoughts, base aspirations, and interpret experiences. To most people, rational existence demands a world view that adds significance to individual actions by placing them in their wider context. In their role as synthesizers, philosophers seek to unite and integrate mankind's specialized knowledges into a unified view of the world.

[8] Cf. Charles D. Marler, *Philosophy and Schooling* (Boston: Allyn and Bacon, Inc., 1975), pp. 5-11; Philip G. Smith, *Philosophy of Education: Introductory Studies* (New York: Harper & Row, 1965), pp. 2-16.

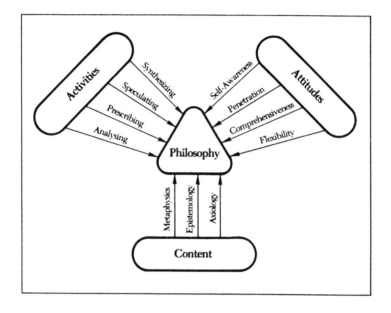

Figure 1
Aspects of Philosophy

The speculative dimension of philosophy is based upon the limitations of human knowledge. There is not enough scientifically verified data to provide a base for action. Furthermore, the most important aspects of human and universal existence are not amenable to scientific treatment. If daily activity is not to be paralyzed, it is necessary to move beyond what can be demonstrated empirically. It is the speculative function of philosophy that allows a rational jump from the known to the unknown, and which permits movement with a relative degree of confidence into the undefined. The alternative to speculation is to be stymied by doubt.

Prescription in philosophy seeks to establish standards for evaluating values in conduct and art. Prescriptions are usually expressed in terms of how people "ought" to act or react in a

5

given situation involving aesthetic judgments or moral alternatives. Intrinsic to prescribing is the task of defining what is meant by good, bad, right, wrong, beautiful, and ugly. The aim of prescriptive philosophy is to discover and illuminate principles for deciding what actions and qualities are most worthwhile. The alternative to prescription is to face every decision-making situation as if it were unique.

Analyzing in philosophy focuses on an examination of human language and our use of it in an attempt to clarify our understanding of problems and how they might be solved. In analysis the philosopher scrutinizes the use of logic in an argument and examines such words as "liberal," "good," "intelligence," and "motivation" in an attempt to evaluate their meanings in varying contexts. The analytic philosopher operates on the assumption that basic misunderstandings in regard to meanings might lie at the root of human problems.

In the twentieth century many philosophers have left the other activities of philosophy and made analysis their only function. This has led to a narrowness that has largely sterilized the discipline and robbed it of its meaning and relevance for the daily activities of social life. Meaningful and vital philosophy contains an interaction and balance of its four central activities.

## Philosophy as an Attitude

Philosophers bring certain ways of thinking to their task. The characteristics of a person who is philosophic-minded may be listed as self-awareness, comprehensiveness, penetration, and flexibility.

Self-awareness entails a commitment to being as honest as possible with one's self in regard to personal biases, assumptions, and prejudices. No one is neutral, and one of the most difficult and elusive activities of human existence is to come to grips with our personal predispositions. It might be said that it is impossible even to begin to arrive at a correct perspective of the world until people realize the color of the glasses they are wearing. Once individuals become aware of the effect of their personal predispositions, they need to take this information into account in both interpretation and communication.

Comprehensiveness involves an inclination toward collecting as much relevant data on a subject as possible from a wide spectrum of sources, rather than being satisfied with a narrow sample. This attitude is related to the synthesizing function of philosophy, in that it is interested in seeing the wholeness of phenomena rather than the parts.

Penetration is a desire that leads a person to go as deeply into a problem as skill, time, and energy allow. It is a squelching of the inclination toward the superficial in favor of a search for basic principles, issues, and solutions.

Flexibility might be thought of as the antithesis of rigidity or "psychological set." The attitude of flexibility is a form of sensitivity that enables one to be able to perceive old problems in new ways. It includes a willingness to restructure ideas in the face of sufficient evidence and the ability to envision viable alternatives to a viewpoint. Flexibility, however, should not be confused with indecisiveness or the inability to make a decision.[9] After careful study, one may decide that a position is the most reasonable and then act in accord with that decision. "The point at issue lies in one's willingness—even readiness—to change that position given sufficient reason."[10]

## Philosophy as Content

It has been noted that philosophy is, in part, an activity and an attitude. If people are involved in such activities as synthesis, speculation, prescription, and analysis; and if they possess the attitudes of self-awareness, comprehensiveness, penetration, and flexibility, then they soon will be confronted with some bedrock questions related to the nature of reality, truth, and value.

The content of philosophy is better seen in the light of questions than in the light of answers. It even can be said that

[9] Smith, *Philosophy of Education*, p. 14.

[10] Marler, *Philosophy and Schooling*, pp. 10-11.

philosophy is the study of questions. Van Cleve Morris has noted that the crux of the matter is asking the "right" questions. By "right" he means questions which are meaningful and relevant—the kind of questions people really want answered and which will make a difference in how they live and work.[11]

There are three fundamental categories around which philosophical content has been organized: (1) *metaphysics*, the study of questions concerning the nature of reality; (2) *epistemology*, the study of the nature of truth and knowledge and how these are attained; and (3) *axiology*, the study of questions of value. A discussion of these three basic categories will form the subject matter of chapter II.

## What Is Education?

"I am not going to get married until after I finish my education," declared a young man to his friends. What did he mean by the term "education"? What was it that he hoped to complete before marriage? Was it education, learning, or schooling? Is there a conceptual difference among these words? If there is, one ought to come to grips with that difference and use the terms with precision. The following discussion will present some distinctions among these concepts and offer definitions[12] that will lead to a better understanding of these related but often confused processes.

In the above illustration the young man evidently meant that he would not get married until he was finished with school. Even though he used the term "education," he was referring to schooling. Schooling might be thought of as attendance at an institution in which teachers and students operate in a prescribed manner. Schooling can be equated with formal education—that education which takes place in a school.

[11] Van Cleve Morris, *Philosophy and the American School* (Boston: Houghton Mifflin Company, 1961), pp. 19-20.

[12] Each of these definitions is presented as *a* possible definition and not *the* definition of the respective term. As such, they may be helpful in stimulating thought and discussion concerning the differences and similarities inherent in these concepts.

Learning proves to be a more difficult concept to define, and different learning theorists have arrived at varying positions concerning the nature of learning. For present purposes, learning may be defined as "the process that produces the capability of exhibiting new or changed human behavior (or which increases the probability that new or changed behavior will be elicited by a relevant stimulus), provided that the new behavior or behavior change cannot be explained on the basis of some other process or experience"—such as aging or fatigue.[13]

From this definition it can be seen that learning is a process that, unlike schooling, is not limited to an institutional context. It is possible to learn individually or with the help of someone else. People can learn in a school, but they can also learn if they have never seen a school. Learning is a lifelong process that may occur at any time and any place.

Education may be seen as a subset of learning. John A. Laska made a helpful distinction between learning and education when he defined education as "the deliberate attempt by the learner or by someone else to *control* (or *guide*, or *direct*, or *influence*, or *manage*) a learning situation in order to bring about the attainment of a desired *learning outcome* (*goal*)."[14]

Education, seen from this perspective, is not limited to schooling or to the traditional curriculum or methodologies of schools. Education, like learning, is a lifelong process that can take place in an infinite variety of circumstances and contexts. On the other hand, education is distinct from the broader concept of learning, since education embodies the idea of deliberate control by the learner or someone else toward a desired goal. Education might be thought of as directed learning, as opposed to nondirected or inadvertent learning.

A fourth term that is sometimes confused with education is "training." The concept (not necessarily the way in which the word is always used) of training may be differentiated from the

---

[13] John A. Laska, *Schooling and Education: Basic Concepts and Problems* (New York: D. Van Nostrand Company, 1976), p. 6. Cf. Ernest R. Hilgard and Gordon H. Bower, *Theories of Learning*, 3d ed. (New York: Appleton-Century-Crofts, 1966), p. 2.

[14] Laska, *Schooling and Education*, p. 7.

9

concept of education on the basis of the development of understanding. Understanding grows as one is led to think reflectively about cause-and-effect relationships rather than just responding to a set of stimuli. A development of understanding is inherent in education, while unreflective responsive activity is generally associated with training. Training can take place on the animal level, while education is essentially a human process. It should be noted that education may at times include some training aspects, since training is a subset of education, just as education is a subset of learning.

Figure 2 illustrates the relationship of learning, education, training, and schooling. Education and training are specialized types of learning, while training, in turn, is a specialized type of education. Schooling is related to these three forms of learning in the sense that inadvertent learning,[15] education, and training

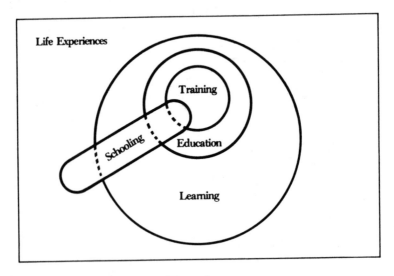

Figure 2
The Relationship of Selected Learning-Related Concepts

[15] In figure 2 the largest circle refers to all learning processes, whereas only that learning outside the education subset represents inadvertent or nondirected learning.

may take place in the context of schooling. Figure 2 illustrates, however, that there are many other life experiences (such as eating lunch or going to the nurse) which take place in school but are not necessarily related to one of the various learning experiences. It may also be seen from figure 2 that most learning, education, and training take place outside the context of a formal school setting.

## The Role of the School in Society

The school is only one of society's agents for learning, education, and training. The family, media, peer group, and church are some of the other institutions that share this responsibility. In fact, the school may even be seen as a minor partner in the educational process, with the family and the media playing the major role in the lives of most children.[16] This vital point should be recognized, even though the treatment of education in this book will tend to use categories that are most often linked with schooling. It should be understood, however, that the "teacher" in the fullest sense of the word may not be an employee of a school system, but may be a broadcaster, parent, pastor, or peer. Likewise, a television program or an individual home has a view of truth and reality and a set of values that lead it to select a certain "curriculum" and teaching methodology as it goes about its educational functions. In what follows, this idea may not

[16] The educational power of the family was highlighted in the influential studies of James Coleman and Christopher Jencks. Implicit in the findings of Coleman and Jencks is that improved families are more crucial to educational outcomes than better schools. Lawrence A. Cremin, in reflecting on these studies, concluded that their message is "not that the school is power*less* but that the family is power*ful*." Complicating the problem is the fact that the Carnegie Council on Children in 1977 found that "by the age of 18, the average American child has spent more time watching television than in school or with his or her parents." (See James S. Coleman et al., *Equality of Educational Opportunity* (Washington, D.C.: U.S. Department of Health, Education, and Welfare, 1966); Christopher Jencks et al., *Inequality: A Reassessment of the Effect of Family and Schooling in America* (New York: Harper and Row, 1972); Lawrence A. Cremin, *Public Education* (New York: Basic Books, 1976), p. 68; Kenneth Keniston et al., *All Our Children: The American Family under Pressure* (New York: Harcourt Brace Jovanovich, 1977), p. 7.)

always be explicitly stated, but it is implicit in the discussion and must be recognized if one is to gain the fullest understanding of education-related processes.

The school exists in a complex educational milieu. To complicate matters, the components of that milieu may not all be espousing the same message in regard to reality, truth, and value. This undoubtedly weakens the impact of the school (as well as the impact of society's other "educators") and gives children a garbled message about their world and what is important in life. It should ever be born in mind that learning, education, training, and schooling take place in this complexity of forces.

# PHILOSOPHIC ISSUES IN EDUCATION      2

**E**ducational philosophy is not distinct from general philosophy; it is general philosophy applied to education as a specific area of human endeavor. Before understanding the structure of educational philosophy, it is imperative to learn something of the basic outline of philosophy. In order to do this, we must examine the categories of metaphysics, epistemology, and axiology.

## Metaphysics

Metaphysics is the branch of philosophy that deals with the nature of reality. "What is ultimately real?" is the basic question asked in the study of metaphysics.

At first glance, it seems too simple a query to waste much time on. After all, average people seem to be quite sure about the "reality" of their world. Just ask them, and they will most likely tell you to open your eyes and look at the clock on the wall, to listen to the sound of a passing train, or to bend down and touch the floor beneath your feet. These things, they claim, are real.

Upon reflection, however, one is tempted to question these initial concepts of reality. For example, what exactly is the reality of the floor upon which you stand? It may seem to have a rather straightforward existence. It is obviously flat, solid, and smooth; it has a particular color; it is composed of an identifiable material, such as wood or concrete; and it supports your weight. At

13

first glance, this is the reality of the floor upon which you are standing. Suppose, however, that a physicist enters the room and is questioned about the reality of the floor. She will reply that the floor is made of molecules; that molecules consist of atoms; atoms of electrons, protons, and neutrons; and these, finally, of electrical energy alone. To her the real floor is a hotbed of molecular motion in which there is more space than matter. A third position on the reality of the floor is offered by a passing chemist, who sees an alternate picture of "floor reality." To him the floor is a body of hydrocarbons associated in a particular way and subject to certain kinds of environmental influences, such as heat, cold, wetness, dryness, and oxidation.

At this point it is evident that the question of reality is not as simplistic as it first appeared. If the reality of a common floor is confusing, what about the larger problems that present themselves as mankind searches for the ultimate reality of the universe?

## Aspects of Metaphysics

A glimpse into the realm of metaphysics can be obtained by examining a list of major questions concerning the nature of reality. It will be seen that the queries of the metaphysician are among the most general questions that can be asked. It is important to realize, however, that the answers to these questions are needed before people can expect to find satisfactory answers to their more specific questions. The complete verification of any particular answer to these questions is beyond the realm of human demonstration. That does not, however, make the discussion of these issues irrelevant or a mere exercise in mental gymnastics, since people, whether they consciously understand it or not, base their daily activities and long-range goals upon a set of metaphysical beliefs. Even people dealing in the answers to more specific questions—physicists or biologists, for example—cannot escape metaphysical problems. Rather, it should be noted that metaphysical constructs lie at the foundation of the modern sciences. "Metaphysics" is a transliteration from the Greek that literally means "beyond physics." It essentially represents the speculative and synthesizing activities of philosophy, and it provides the theoretical framework that allows scientists to create world views and develop hypotheses that can be tested according to their basic assumptions. Thus, theories of science are ultimately related to theories of reality, and the philosophy of science underlies scientific experimentation in much the same way that philosophy of education forms the foundation of educational practice. It should be recognized that scientists are at times tempted to make interpretations that go beyond the "facts" of the answers to their relatively narrow questions and to invade the realm of supplying metaphysical answers. Such is the position of scientists who make positive statements about either creationism or evolution. They have gone beyond their experimental facts and assumed the role of metaphysicians. This may be all right in itself, as long as both they and their students consciously realize that they have exited the realm of science and entered that more basic world of metaphysics.

Metaphysical questions may be divided into four subsets. First, there is the cosmological aspect. Cosmology consists in the study of theories about the origin, nature, and development of the universe as an orderly system. "How did the universe originate and develop?" is a cosmological question. People have answered that question in a variety of ways, and their answers can be viewed as points on a continuum with design and accident as its polar extremes. Another cosmological inquiry is in regard to the purposefulness of the universe. Is there a purpose toward which the universe is tending? Affirmative replies to this query are referred to as being teleological. Certain religious philosophies emphasize the purposefulness of both history and the cosmos. On the other hand, there are many philosophic schemes that are prone to accept randomness or circularity in history. Two other widely discussed cosmological issues center around the nature of time and space.

A second metaphysical aspect is the theological. Theology is that part of religious theory that has to do with conceptions of and about God. Is there a God? If so, is there one or more than one? What are the attributes of God? If God is both all good and all powerful, how is it that evil exists? Are there such beings as

15

angels? Are there evil powers? If so, what is their relationship to God? These and similar questions have been debated throughout the history of mankind. People answer these questions in a variety of ways. *Atheists* claim that there is no God, while *pantheists* posit that God and the universe are identical—all is God, and God is all. *Deists* view God as the maker of nature and moral laws, but assert that God exists apart from, and is not interested in, mankind and the physical universe. On the other hand, *theists* believe in a personal creator God. *Polytheism* is opposed to *monotheism* in regard to the question of the number of gods. Polytheism holds that the deity should be thought of as plural, while monotheism holds that there is one God.

A third aspect of metaphysics is the anthropological. Anthropology deals with the study of mankind. The anthropological aspect of philosophy is a unique category, since, unlike other areas of human investigation, mankind is both the subject and the object of inquiry. When people philosophize about mankind, they are speaking about themselves. The anthropological aspect of philosophy asks questions like the following: What is the relation between mind and body? Is there interaction between mind and body? Is mind more fundamental than body, with body depending on mind, or vice versa? What is mankind's moral status? Are people born good, evil, or morally neutral? To what extent are individuals free? Do they have free will, or are their thoughts and actions determined by their environment and inheritance? Does an individual have a soul? If so, what is it? People have obviously adopted different positions on these questions, and those positions are reflected in their political, social, religious, and educational practices and designs.

The fourth aspect of metaphysics is the ontological. Ontology is the study of the nature of existence, or what it means for anything to be. J. Donald Butler has coined the word *"isology"* as a synonym for "ontology," since the ontological task "is to determine what we mean when we say that something *is.*"[1] There are several questions which are central to ontology: Is basic reality

[1] J. Donald Butler, *Four Philosophies and Their Practice in Education and Religion*, 3d ed. (New York: Harper & Row, 1968), p. 21.

found in matter or physical energy (the world we can sense), or is it found in spirit or spiritual energy? Is it composed of one element (e.g., matter or spirit), or two (e.g., matter and spirit), or many? Is reality orderly and lawful in itself, or is it merely orderable by mankind? Is it fixed and stable, or is change its central feature? Is this reality friendly, unfriendly, or neutral in regard to humanity?

## Metaphysics and Education

Even a cursory glance at either historical or contemporary societies will indicate the impact of the cosmological, theological, anthropological, and ontological aspects of metaphysics upon their social, religious, political, economic, and scientific beliefs and practices. People everywhere assume answers to these questions and then turn around and operate in their daily lives on those assumptions. There is no escape from metaphysical decisions, unless one chooses merely to vegetate—and even that decision, in itself, would be a metaphysical decision about the nature and function of humanity.

Education, like other human activities, cannot escape the realm of metaphysics. Metaphysics, the study of ultimate reality, is central to any concept of education, because it is important that the educational program of the school be based upon fact and reality rather than fancy, illusion, or imagination. Varying metaphysical beliefs lead to differing educational approaches and even separate systems of education.

Why is it that Jews, Christians, and other special interest groups spend millions of dollars each year to provide private systems of education when free public schooling is widely available? It is because of metaphysical beliefs regarding the nature of ultimate reality, the role of human beings in the cosmos, and the significance of life. Men and women, at their deepest level, are motivated by metaphysical beliefs. They are willing to live and die for these convictions, and they desire to create educational environments in which these most basic beliefs will be taught to their children.

Later in this book it will be seen that metaphysical beliefs have a direct impact upon such educational issues as the most important content for the curriculum, what educational systems should attempt to do for both individuals and societies, and the role of teachers as they relate to learners. The anthropological aspect of metaphysics is especially important for educators of all persuasions. After all, they are dealing with malleable human beings at one of the most impressionable stages of their lives. Views on the nature and potential of students lie at the very foundation of the educational process. Every educator must of necessity have some conception of the nature of human beings, their personal and social needs, and some image of the ideal person. The very purpose of education in all philosophies is closely related to these views. Thus, anthropological considerations lie extremely close to aims in education. D. Elton Trueblood put it nicely when he asserted that "until we are clear on what man is we shall not be clear about much else." One spin-off of the centrality of anthropological considerations in education is the role of psychological study in the training of teachers. The same is true of sociology, but to a lesser extent in most teacher-training programs.[2]

It makes a great deal of difference in education if a student is viewed as Desmond Morris's "naked ape" or as a child of God. Likewise, it is important to know whether children are essentially good, as is asserted of Rousseau's Emile, or whether their goodness has been radically twisted. Variation in anthropological positions will lead to significantly different approaches to the educational process. Other examples of the impact of metaphysics upon education will become evident further on in our study of educational philosophy.

---

[2] Paul Nash, Andreas M. Kazamias, and Henry J. Perkinson, *The Educated Man: Studies in the History of Educational Thought* (New York: John Wiley & Sons, 1966); Paul Nash, *Models of Man: Explorations in the Western Educational Tradition* (New York: John Wiley & Sons, 1968); David Elton Trueblood, *Philosophy of Religion* (New York: Harper & Row, 1957), p. xiv.

# Epistemology

The branch of philosophy that studies the nature, sources, and validity of knowledge is epistemology. It seeks to answer such questions as "What is true?" and "How do we know?" Due to the fact that the study of epistemology deals with such issues as the dependability of knowledge and the propriety of various methods of reaching warrantable truth, it stands—with metaphysics—at the very center of the educative process.

## Dimensions of Knowledge

*Can reality be known?* This is a logical question with which to begin the epistemological venture, since it demonstrates the close connection between epistemology and metaphysics. *Skepticism*, in its narrow sense, is the position claiming that it is impossible to gain knowledge and that the search for truth is vain. This thought was well expressed by Gorgias (c. 483-376 B.C.), the Greek Sophist who asserted that nothing exists, and that if it did, we could not know it. A full-blown skepticism would make intelligent and consistent action impossible. Skepticism, in its broader sense, is often used to denote the attitude of questioning any assumption or conclusion until it can be subjected to rigorous examination. A term closely related to skepticism is "agnosticism." *Agnosticism* is a profession of ignorance, especially in reference to the existence or nonexistence of God, rather than a positive denial of any valid knowledge.

Most people claim that reality can be known. Once they have taken that position, however, they must decide through what sources reality may be known, and they must have some conception of how to judge the validity of their knowledge.

*Is truth relative or absolute?* Is all truth subject to change? Is it possible that what is true today may be false tomorrow? Truths that would answer yes to the previous questions are relative. Absolute Truth refers to that Truth which is eternally and universally true irrespective of time or place. If there is that kind of Truth in the universe, then it would certainly be helpful to discover it and place it at the very center of the school curriculum.

19

*Is knowledge subjective or objective?* This question is closely related to the relativity of truth. Van Cleve Morris has noted that there are three basic positions on the objectivity of knowledge. First, some hold that knowledge is something that comes to us from the "outside" and is inserted into our minds and nervous systems in much the same way iron ore is dumped into a ship. Morris claims that mathematicians and physical scientists often see knowledge in this light. Second, others believe that knowers contribute something in this engagement of themselves with the world in such a way as to be partially responsible for the structure of their knowledge. People in the social and behavioral sciences have often tended to see knowledge in this manner. A third and final viewpoint is that we exist as "pure subjects," who become the manufacturers of truth rather than either its recipients or participants. This position, notes Morris, is most generally held in such areas as art, literature, and music.[3] Later it will be observed that the various philosophical schools tend to align themselves with one or another of these viewpoints on the objectivity of truth and knowledge.

*Is there truth independent of human experience?* This question is basic to epistemology. It can best be viewed in terms of *a priori* and *a posteriori* knowledge. *A priori* knowledge refers to truth that some thinkers claim is built into the very fabric of reality. It is independent of human knowers and is true whether any human knows and accepts it or not. This type of truth is said to exist prior to human experience of it and is independent of human awareness. An example of *a priori* knowledge is the ratio existing between the circumference and diameter of a circle ($\pi$). This relationship is a part of the very nature of circles. On the other hand, the relation existing between one circle and another is not given. One circle may be larger than the other, they may be in the same or different planes, or they may be concentric. Whatever knowledge one may have of the relationship of these two circles requires human experience for verification. Whatever knowledge is attained regarding their relationship is *a posteriori*

---

[3] Van Cleve Morris, *Philosophy and the American School*, p. 118.

—it is posterior to human experience of it and is dependent on human awareness.

Traditional philosophies have upheld the superiority of *a priori* knowledge, since, they claim, it is thought to represent the fixed and permanent world that is uncontaminated by human knowers. Modern philosophies have reversed this order and claim the superiority of *a posteriori* knowledge. In fact, some of them deny the existence of *a priori* knowledge.

## Sources of Knowledge

*The senses.* Empiricism is the view that knowledge is obtained through the senses, that people form pictures of the world around them by seeing, hearing, smelling, feeling, and tasting. Empirical knowledge is built into the very nature of human experience. Individuals may walk out of doors on a spring day and see the beauty of the landscape, hear the song of a bird, feel the warm rays of the sun, and smell the fragrance of the blossoms. They "know" that it is spring because of the messages received through their senses. This knowledge is composed of ideas formed in accordance with observed data. Sensory knowing among humans is immediate and universal, and in many ways it forms the basis for much of our knowledge.

The presence of sensory data cannot be denied. Most twentieth-century people accept it at face value as representing "reality." The danger hidden in a naive acceptance of this approach is that our senses have been demonstrated to be both incomplete and undependable. For example, most people have been confronted with the sensation of seeing a stick that looks bent when partially submerged in water but appears to be straight when examined in the air. Fatigue, frustration, and common colds also distort and limit sensory perception. In addition, it comes as no surprise that there are sound and light waves beyond the range of unaided human perception. Humans have invented scientific instruments to extend the range of their senses, but it is impossible to ascertain the exact dependability of these instruments, since we do not know the total effect of the human mind in recording, interpreting, and distorting sensual

21

perception. Confidence in these instruments is built upon speculative metaphysical theories whose validity has been reinforced by experimentation in which predictions have been verified in terms of a theoretical construct.

In short, sensory knowledge is built upon assumptions that must be accepted by faith in the dependability of our sensory mechanisms. The advantage of empirical knowledge is that many sensory experiences and experiments are open to both replication and public examination.

*Revelation.* Revealed knowledge has been of prime importance in the field of religion. It differs from all other sources of knowledge by presupposing a transcendent supernatural reality that breaks into the natural order. Revelation is God's communication concerning the divine will. Believers in revelation hold that this form of knowledge has the distinct advantage of being an omniscient source of information that is not obtainable through other epistemological methods. The truth gained through this source is believed to be absolute and uncontaminated. On the other hand, it is generally realized that distortion of revealed truth can take place in the process of human interpretation. Some people hold that a major disadvantage of revealed knowledge is that it must be accepted by faith and cannot be proved or disproved empirically.

*Authority.* Authoritative knowledge is accepted as true because it comes from experts or has been sanctified over time as tradition. In the classroom the most common source of information is some authority, such as a textbook, teacher, or reference work.

Authority as a source of knowledge has its values as well as its dangers. Civilization would certainly be in a state of stagnation if each individual were unwilling to accept any statement unless he or she had personally verified it through direct, firsthand experience. The acceptance of authoritative knowledge generally saves time and enhances social and scientific progress. On the other hand, this form of knowledge is only as valid as the assumptions upon which it stands. If authoritative knowledge is built upon a foundation of incorrect assumptions, then that knowledge will of necessity be distorted.

*Reason.* The view that reasoning, thought, or logic is the central factor in knowledge is known as rationalism. The rationalist, in emphasizing humanity's power of thought and what the mind contributes to knowledge, is likely to claim that the senses alone cannot provide us with universally valid judgments that are consistent with one another. From this perspective the sensations and experiences which we gain through our senses are the raw materials of knowledge. These sensations must be organized by the mind into a meaningful system before they become knowledge.

Rationalism, in its less extreme form, claims that mankind has the power to know with certainty various truths about the universe which the senses alone cannot give. For example, if x is equal to y, and y is equal to z, then x is equal to z. It is possible to know that this is true quite independently of any actual instances or experiences and that it applies to boxes, triangles, and other concrete objects in the universe. In its more extreme form, rationalism claims that mankind is capable of arriving at irrefutable knowledge independently of sense experience.

Formal logic is a tool used by rationalists. Systems of logic have the advantage of having internal consistency, but they face the danger of not being related to the external world. Logical systems of thought are only as valid as the premises upon which they are built.

*Intuition.* The direct apprehension of knowledge that is not the result of conscious reasoning or of immediate sense perception is called "intuition." In the literature dealing with intuition we often find such expressions as "immediate feeling of certainty" and "imagination touched with conviction." Intuition occurs beneath the "threshhold of consciousness." It is often experienced as a "sudden flash of insight." Many students have had such experiences while working out mathematical problems for which they obtain the answer before they have been able to work through the steps of the problem. Intuition is perhaps the

23

most personal way of knowing. It is a direct apprehension of knowledge accompanied by an intense feeling of conviction that one has discovered what he or she is looking for. Intuition has been claimed, under varying circumstances, as a source for both religious and secular knowledge.

The weakness or danger of intuition is that it does not appear to be a safe method of obtaining knowledge when used alone. It goes astray very easily and may lead to absurd claims unless it is controlled by or checked against other methods of knowing. Intuitive knowledge, however, has the distinct advantage of being able to leap over the limitations of human experience.

*The complementary nature of knowledge sources.* There is no one source of knowledge that supplies mankind with all knowledge. The various sources should be seen in a complementary relationship rather than one of antagonism. It is true, however, that most thinkers choose one source as being more basic than the others. This most basic source is then used as a background against which other means of obtaining knowledge are evaluated. For example, in the modern world empirical knowledge generally is seen as the most basic source. Most people hold any purported knowledge suspect if it does not agree with scientific theory. By way of contrast, Western society during the Middle Ages saw rationalism and revelation as the major providers of the framework within which other sources of knowledge could be tested.

## Validity of Knowledge[4]

In mankind's recorded history it is evident that many beliefs once accepted as true were later discovered to be false. How can one say that some beliefs are true while others are false? What criteria can be used? Can we ever be certain that the truth has been discovered? Most people agree that tradition, instinct, and

[4] Cf. Harold H. Titus and Marilyn S. Smith, *Living Issues in Philosophy*, 6th ed. (New York: D. Van Nostrand Co., 1974), pp. 266-73. See also John S. Brubacher, *Modern Philosophies of Education*, 4th ed. (New York: McGraw-Hill Book Co., 1969), pp. 227-30.

strong feelings are inadequate tests of truth. Universal agreement is also suspect, since all humans may have the same inherent shortcomings. Philosophers, in the main, have relied on three tests of truth—the correspondence, coherence, and pragmatic theories.

*The correspondence theory.* The correspondence theory is a test which uses agreement with "fact" as a standard of judgment. According to this theory, truth is faithfulness to objective reality. For example, the statement "There is a lion in the classroom" can be verified by empirical investigation. If a judgment corresponds with the facts, it is true; if not, it is false. This test of truth is often held by those working in the sciences.

Critics of the correspondence theory have put forth three main objections. First, they ask: "How can we compare our ideas with reality, since we know only our own experiences and cannot get outside of our experiences so that we can compare our ideas with reality in its 'pure' state?" Second, they note that the theory of correspondence also seems generally to assume that our sense data are clear and accurate. And, third, the critics point out that the theory is inadequate because we have ideas that have no concrete existence outside the area of human thought with which we can make comparisons. Many mental constructs in ethics, logic, and mathematics fall into this category.

*The coherence theory.* This theory places its trust in the consistency or harmony of all one's judgments. According to this test, a judgment is true if it is consistent with other judgments that have previously been accepted as true. The proponents of the coherence theory of truth point out, for example, that a statement is often judged to be true or false on the ground that it is or is not in harmony with what has already been decided to be true. This test of validity has generally been held by those who deal with abstract ideas and uplift intellectualism, as opposed to those who deal with the material aspects of reality.

Critics of the coherence approach have noted that false systems of thought can be just as internally consistent as true systems. They claim, therefore, that the theory falls short of what is needed because it does not distinguish between consistent truth and consistent error.

25

*The pragmatic theory.* There is a large group of modern philosophers who claim that there is no such thing as static or absolute truth. Pragmatists (to be discussed in chapter IV) reject the correspondence theory due to their belief that people know only their experiences. They also dismiss the coherence theory because it is formal and rationalistic in a world in which we can know nothing about "substances," "essences," and "ultimate realities." Pragmatists see the test of truth in its utility, workability, or satisfactory consequences. In the thinking of John Dewey and William James, truth is what works.

Traditionalists have seen dangers in this test of truth, since it leads to relativism in the sense that there can be one truth for you and another for me. Critics also assert that "what works" in the limited range of human experience may be delusive when measured against what they see as an external reality built into the very essence of the universe.

## Epistemology and Education

Epistemology, like metaphysics, stands at the base of human thought and activity. Educational systems deal in knowledge, and therefore epistemology is a primary determinant of educational beliefs and practices. Epistemology makes a direct impact upon education in many ways. For example, assumptions about the importance of the various sources of knowledge will certainly be reflected in curricular emphases. A school system that is based on naturalistic premises and holds that science is the primary source of knowledge will undoubtedly have a curriculum and curricular materials that differ substantially in some areas from those of a religious school that holds that revelation is a source of certain knowledge. Epistemological assumptions concerning the communication of knowledge from one person or thing to another person will also impact upon teaching methodologies and the function of the teacher in the educative context. Educators must understand their epistemological presuppositions before they will be able to operate effectively.

## The Metaphysical-Epistemological Dilemma

At this point it is evident that mankind is suspended, so to speak, in midair both metaphysically and epistemologically. Our problem is that it is not possible to make statements about reality without first having a theory for arriving at truth; and, on the other hand, a theory of truth cannot be developed without first having a concept of reality. We are caught in the web of circularity.

Through the study of basic questions, people are forced to realize their smallness and helplessness in the universe. They must realize that nothing can be known for certain in the sense of final and ultimate proof that is open and acceptable to all people.[5] Every person—the skeptic and the agnostic, the scientist and the businessman, the Hindu and the Christian—lives by a faith. The acceptance of a particular position in metaphysics and epistemology is a "faith-choice" made by individuals, and it entails a commitment to a way of life.

The circular nature of the reality-truth dilemma is certainly not the most comforting aspect of philosophical thought, but since it does exist, we are obligated to make ourselves aware of it. Of course, this whole problem comes as no surprise to mature scientists who have come to grips with the limitations of their art and the philosophy upon which it is built. Neither does it pose a threat to believers in certain religious persuasions, who have traditionally seen their basic beliefs in terms of personal choice, faith, and commitment. The whole problem, however, does come as a great shock to the average individual who has been conditioned to place unconditional faith in modern science.

---

[5] D. Elton Trueblood has spoken to this point: "It is now widely recognized that absolute proof is something which the human being does not and cannot have. This follows necessarily from the twin fact that deductive reasoning cannot have certainty about its premises and that inductive reasoning cannot have certainty about its conclusions. The notion that, in natural science, we have both certainty and absolute proof is simply one of the superstitions of our age." *A Place to Stand* (New York: Harper & Row, 1969), p. 22; for a fuller discussion on the limits of proof, see Trueblood, *General Philosophy*, pp. 92-111.

The conclusion of the metaphysical-epistemological dilemma is that all persons live by faith in the basic beliefs they have chosen. Different individuals have made different faith-choices on the metaphysical-epistemological continuum and therefore have varying philosophic positions.

The remainder of this book will examine the educational implications of distinctive philosophical choices. Before moving to that material, however, we will need to explore a third major area of philosophical content.

# Axiology

Axiology is the branch of philosophy that seeks to answer the question: "What is of value?" People's interest in values stems from the fact that they are valuing beings. Humans desire some things more than others—they have preferences. Rational individual and social life is based upon a system of values. Value systems are not universally agreed upon, and different positions on the questions of metaphysics and epistemology determine different systems of value, because axiological systems are built upon conceptions of reality and truth.

The question of values deals with notions of what a person or a society conceives of as being good or preferable. A problem arises when two different conceptions of good or value are held by the same society or person. For example, a society may define a good as clean air and water. Yet that same society may turn around and pollute the earth in its acquisition of another good—money and material things. In such a case there is a clear tension in values—a tension between what people say they value and what they act out in their daily life. Thus, one might ask, "Which do they really value—what they say or what they do?"

Charles Morris has labeled the values that people verbalize, but may not actualize, as "conceived values." Those that they act upon he has referred to as "operative values."[6] Van Cleve

---

[6] Charles Morris, *Varieties of Human Value* (Chicago: The University of Chicago Press, 1956), pp 10-11.

Morris went one step beyond the problem of conceived and operative values by claiming that this whole problem is actually of mere "tactical" importance when compared to the "strategic" seriousness of discovering "what we *ought* to prefer."[7] In other words, he is claiming that the most crucial value issue for educators is determining what people ought to prefer rather than defining and clarifying those preferences that they act out or verbalize.

Axiology, like metaphysics and epistemology, stands at the very foundation of the educational process. A major aspect of education is the development of preferences. The classroom is an axiological theater in which teachers cannot hide their moral selves. In the area of axiology, teachers constantly instruct, by their actions, groups of highly impressionable young people, who assimilate and imitate their teachers' value structures to a significant extent. Axiology has two main branches—ethics and aesthetics.

## Ethics

Ethics is the study of moral values and conduct. It seeks to answer such questions as "What should I do?," "What is the good life for all people?," and "What is good conduct?" Ethical theory is concerned with providing right values as the foundation for right actions. Harold Titus and Marilyn Smith claim that the question of morality is the central issue of our time.[8] World society has made unprecedented technological advances, but has not advanced significantly, if at all, in ethical and moral conceptions. In 1952 George S. Counts noted that Western society had become so enraptured by technological advance that it tended to conceive of human progress largely in technological terms. Progress had come to mean more gadgets, more labor-saving devices,

---

[7] Van Cleve Morris, *Philosophy and the American School*, p. 221.

[8] Titus and Smith, *Living Issues in Philosophy*, p. 115.

more speed in transportation, and more material comforts. "We are learning today, to our sorrow," said Counts, "that this advance, when not accompanied by equally profound reconstruction in the realms of understanding and value, of customs and institutions, of attitudes and loyalties, can bring trouble and disaster."[9] A decade later, writing on the same topic, he quoted Wernher Von Braun, the authority on rockets, as warning: "If the world's ethical standards fail to rise with the advance of our technological revolution, we shall perish."[10]

The study of ethics is crucial in a world civilization that has the power to destroy the natural order through "peaceful" industrial processes or to obliterate more violently the present culture through nuclear warfare. Science and technology in themselves are morally neutral, but the uses to which they are put involve ethical considerations.

Both as a society and as individuals we exist in a world in which meaningful ethical decisions cannot be avoided. Due to this fact, it is impossible to escape the teaching of ethical concepts in the school. Of course, one may choose to remain silent on these issues. That silence, however, is not neutrality—it is merely supporting the ethical *status quo.*

Ethical conceptions will enter the classroom in one form or another. The problem is that people differ in their ethical bases and they feel quite strongly about having their children "indoctrinated" in a moral view that is alien to their fundamental beliefs. This issue is more of a problem in public school systems than in private or parochial schools, since the latter are generally established to teach a particular world view to a largely homogeneous group of pupils.

The following questions highlight the ethical problems that divide people:

- Are ethical standards and moral values absolute or relative?

[9] George S. Counts, *Education and American Civilization* (New York: Teachers College, Columbia University, Bureau of Publications, 1952), p. 130.

[10] George S. Counts, *Education and the Foundations of Human Freedom* (Pittsburgh: University of Pittsburgh Press, 1962), pp. 27-28.

- Do universal moral values exist?
- Does the end ever justify the means?
- Can morality be separated from religion?
- Who or what forms the basis of ethical authority?

## Aesthetics

Aesthetics is the realm of value that searches for the principles governing the creation and appreciation of beauty and art. Aesthetics deals with the theoretical aspects of art in its widest sense and should not be confused with actual works of art or the technical criticism of them. Perhaps aesthetics ranks as the most controversial human study. If you want to get certain segments of any population excited, just begin to make authoritative judgments about the value of specific forms of literature, music, and visual art. Aesthetics is a realm of theory that relates closely to imagination and creativity, and it therefore tends to become highly personal and subjective.

Historians of past civilizations have usually considered artistic accomplishments to be an important mark of cultural development. By way of contrast, it should be recognized that some modern societies, such as the United States, have given primary importance to utilitarian and material concerns. Art "bakes no bread" for competitive individuals seeking to get ahead in the world, and it may not be seen as important by a culture embroiled in a race for survival in the technological and military spheres. As a result, artistic works and aesthetic appreciation have found a rather low place in the hierarchy of American education. This priority was highlighted by the influential Conant Report, which did not recommend art as a requirement for high-school graduation. More recently, the National Commission on Excellence in Education also gave the arts only marginal recognition in its recommended curriculum.[11]

---

[11] John Martin Rich, *Education and Human Values* (Reading, Mass.: Addison-Wesley Publishing Co., 1968), pp. 125, 146. See also James B. Conant, *The American High School Today* (New York: McGraw-Hill Book Co., 1959); National Commission on Excellence in Education, *A Nation at Risk: The Imperative for Educational Reform* (Washington, D.C.: U.S. Government Printing Office, 1983), p. 26.

One must realize, however, that aesthetic valuation is a part of daily experience and cannot be avoided. The aesthetic experience often leads to a heightened sense of perception, an ability to apprehend new meanings, an elevation of feeling, and a broadened sensitivity. In one sense, the aesthetic experience is tied to the cognitive world of intellectual understanding; but in another sense, it soars beyond the cognitive into the affective realm with its focus on feeling and emotion. The aesthetic experience enables people to move beyond the limits imposed by purely rational thought and the weakness of human language. A picture, song, or story may create an impression in a person that could never be conveyed through logical argument. Many great teachers have relied on aesthetic dynamics by teaching through stories.

Human beings are aesthetic beings, and it is just as impossible to avoid teaching aesthetics in the school, home, media, or church as it is to avoid inculcating ethical values. If educators do not consciously face up to their aesthetic responsibilities, they will make aesthetic impressions upon their students unconsciously and uncritically. Areas of aesthetic importance in the school are usually thought of in terms of art, music, and literature classes. These aspects of the formal educational experience are certainly important in developing creativity and appreciation and in heightening a child's sensitivity to emotions and feelings, but perhaps the aesthetic experience is broader than these formal experiences. Some philosophers and educators believe that the school and other educational agencies also have a responsibility to help students see the aesthetic dimension in the educational environment in such areas as architecture, the school grounds, personal neatness, and the neatly written paper. Aesthetics permeates the educational atmosphere, and the questions of "What is beautiful?" and "What should I like?" form one more part of the philosophic platform underlying education.

There are several issues that lay the basis for differences in aesthetic theory and choice. In evaluating these issues, individuals should keep in mind that aesthetic belief is directly related to other aspects of their philosophy. For example, if subjectivity and randomness are accepted in epistemology and metaphysics, they will be reflected in both aesthetics and ethics. Aesthetics is not a realm divorced from the rest of life. People's aesthetic values are a reflection of their total philosophy. The following issues form the basis for divergent aesthetic positions:

- Should art be imitative and representative, or should it be the product of the private creative imagination?
- Should the subject matter of artistic forms deal with the good in life only, or should it also include the ugly and grotesque?
- What is "good" art? By what standard, if any, can art be labeled "beautiful" or "ugly"?
- Should art have a social function and message, or should its meaning remain forever private to its creator?
- Should there be art for art's sake, or must it have a practical significance?
- Does beauty inhere in the art object itself, or is beauty supplied by the eye of the beholder?

## Axiology and Education

The study of axiology has always been important, but it has a special relevance for educators who live in the last quarter of the twentieth century. The last century has seen an unprecedented upheaval in value structures, and today we live at a time when mankind's axiological position might best be described by the words "deterioration" and "flux."

John Gardner, Secretary of Health, Education, and Welfare under President Lyndon Johnson, pointed out that a century ago it took a great deal of courage to become a rebel and attack certain dysfunctional aspects of a rigid social system. He noted, however, that these rebels were often highly moral people who were seeking a deeper level of value than could be seen from the surface. His conclusion was that the superficial has been destroyed and that the time has come to quit "pulverizing the fragments" and to begin asking what we intend to do "to protect ourselves from the elements." Gardner made a crucial observation in noting that "once it was the skeptic, the critic of the *status quo*, who had to make a great effort. Today the skeptic is the *status quo*. The one who must make the effort is the man who seeks to create a new moral order."[12]

E. F. Schumacher demonstrated similar insight when he observed that the person "who conceived the idea that 'morality is bunk' did so with a mind well-stocked with moral ideas." He continued by pointing out that many of our generation no longer have a mind well-stocked with moral ideas: instead, such minds are well-stocked with the nineteenth-century concept that "morality is bunk." Schumacher concluded by calling for a reconstruction of our thought, so that we can focus upon the deepest problems of our age. Without such a re-emphasis of axiological concerns, he postulated, education will prove to be an agent of destruction rather than a constructive resource.[13]

## Philosophic Issues and Educational Goals and Practices

Chapter I described education as a deliberate process that has a desired goal. If this is the case, then educators must have some basis for arriving at a conception of that goal. Concern with a goal presupposes a world view or a philosophical viewpoint that involves a set of beliefs in the nature of reality, the essence of truth, and a basis for forming values. As noted above, concepts of reality, truth, and value are the "stuff" of philosophy. Philosophy, therefore, is a basic constituent in the foundation of educational practice.

Figure 3 illustrates the fact that there is a definite relationship between philosophic beliefs and educational practices. For example, a distinct metaphysical and epistemological viewpoint will lead to a value orientation. That value orientation, in conjunction with its corresponding view of reality and truth, will determine the goals that will be deliberately aimed at in the educational

[12] John W. Gardner, *Self-Renewal: The Individual in the Innovative Society* (New York: Harper & Row, 1964), pp. 120-22.

[13] E. F. Schumacher, *Small Is Beautiful: Economics as if People Mattered* (New York: Harper & Row, 1973), pp. 93-94.

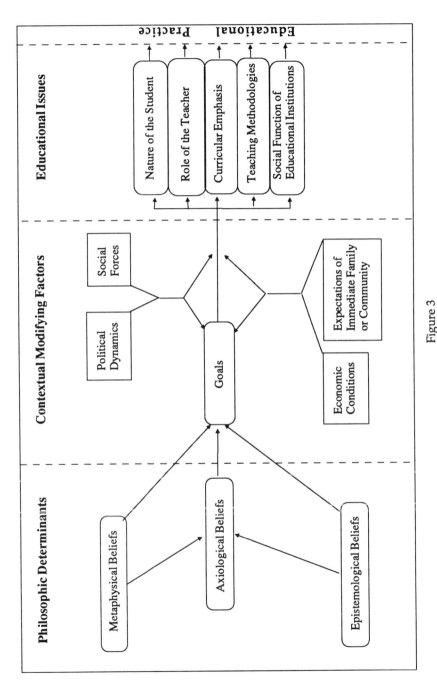

Figure 3
The Relationship of Philosophy to Educational Practice

process. The goals, in turn, will suggest preferred methods and curricular emphases. Chapters III and IV illustrate that varying positions on philosophic issues often lead to different educational practices when educators are consistent with their beliefs. This does not imply that different philosophic beliefs will always lead to different practices, since people may arrive at the same destination from different starting points. Nor does it mean that educators holding similar philosophic beliefs will choose the same practical applications. The point to note is that it is important for educators to choose, select, and develop practices that are in harmony with their beliefs.

It is also important to recognize that philosophy is not the sole determinant of specific educational practices. Figure 3 points out that elements in the everyday world play a significant role in shaping educational practice. For instance, many factors— including political forces, economic conditions, the needs of the labor market, and the social conceptions of a particular population—impact upon educational practice. Philosophy might be seen as providing the basic boundaries for preferred educational practices for any group in society. Within these boundaries adjustments are made for particular situations in the everyday world. Parochial and private education sometimes arises when a subset of the population establishes a different set of philosophic foundations and educational boundaries from those of the larger culture. In such situations an observer would expect to find some basic differences between the public school system and the private alternative, since they are built upon different belief systems.

## Perspective

Chapters I and II have indicated that the study of the philosophy of education is to help educators avoid the "mindless" fallacy of neglecting to root their educational practices in their basic beliefs. Education has been defined as a deliberate process that is goal-oriented. Philosophy has been set forth as a threefold entity (an activity, an attitude, and a body of content) that gives direction to education, since educational goals have a relationship to the metaphysical, epistemological, and axiological content of one's philosophy. It has also been noted that education and its related learning processes take place in a complex milieu in which the school is one of many dynamic forces. Philosophic beliefs determine the basic goals of education, but social dynamics modify both educational goals and practices.

Perhaps the central message of chapters I and II is that educators must seek to establish educational environments and practices that are in harmony with their basic beliefs. The next four chapters will examine some traditional and modern approaches to linking philosophy and education.

# TRADITIONAL PHILOSOPHIES AND EDUCATION     3

C hapter II examined three central philosophic issues—
metaphysics, epistemology, and axiology. Not everyone answers the questions spawned by these issues in the same
way. Different approaches to these questions give rise to various
"schools" of philosophy, such as idealism, realism, neo-
scholasticism, pragmatism, and existentialism. These differences
in philosophic belief lead to variance in educational theory and
practice. There is a direct relationship between people's basic
beliefs and how they view such educational components as the
nature of the student, the role of the teacher, the best curricular
emphasis, the most efficient instructional methods, and the social
function of the school. The remainder of this book will examine
the connection between philosophy and education. The present
chapter will discuss the relationship in terms of traditional philosophy, while chapter IV will perform the same task in the light
of modern philosophy. Chapter V will examine contemporary
educational theories, and will, at first glance, look like a departure from the basic principle of organization. Upon a second
viewing, however, these theories will be seen as educational extensions of the philosophic positions presented in chapters III
and IV. Chapter VI will discuss analytic philosophy. The last
chapter will highlight the building of a personal philosophy of
education.

# The Function and Limitation of Labels

The next two chapters will be using labels for groups of philosophers who approach the major issues of philosophy in basically the same manner. For example, some philosophers will be called pragmatists, while others will be referred to as idealists. At the outset it is important that the reader understand the limitations of any labeling system. First, any system for the classification of philosophic schools is, at best, only loosely accurate. One should not get the idea that philosophers may all be neatly categorized into five or six little boxes and that each of these groups is completely distinct from the rest. The schools of philosophy might rather be seen as points on several continua on which there are differences but also agreements and overlapping. Therefore, no one classification is ever totally satisfactory. Second, too much reliance upon labels may prove to be a substitute for thought about the significance of the differences between the systems and the variations between philosophers within a particular "school." Gaining an idea of the significance of the labels is the beginning rather than the end of understanding the nature of philosophy. Third, labels must be seen for what they are—a simplification of a complex field, so that neophytes will be able to find a starting place for their understanding.

Despite the limitations inherent in the use of labels, they still have a great deal of value. For one thing, the human mind demands classification systems. When faced with large banks of random data, the mind begins to search for understanding by dividing that data into manageable segments on the basis of distinctions and likenesses. It then applies names to the groups, so that the name or label is symbolic of a whole set of characteristics and affinities. Labels, therefore, help us focus on meaningful aspects and divisions of a topic. Thus, a first function of labels is to serve as handles by which we can get hold of an area of thought; they help us gain control over a subject and clear up what would otherwise be a blur. A second function of labels is to aid us in evaluating new material in the framework of what we already know. In this role, labels not only help us establish a knowledge system, but they also help us extend and enrich it. Used in a functional way, labels act as a general guide to help us make sense out of a complex universe. Labels become dysfunctional when they obscure the complexity that lies behind them and thus become a substitute for thinking rather than a tool of intelligence.

Labels have been used in this book to help the beginning student in educational philosophy see how basic differences regarding the nature of reality, truth, and value often lead to differing educational practices. This understanding is crucial, since it is imperative that our educational practices be in harmony with our basic beliefs. It is unfortunate that this is often not the case among educational practitioners. As a result, their practices all too often do not implement advancement toward their stated goals. It is such a state of affairs that has fostered a "bandwagon mentality" among many educators and has caused them to adopt educational innovations as panaceas before they have evaluated them in terms of basic beliefs and desired end products. This frantic activity is what has brought the charge of "mindlessness" against the educational establishment. Educators must realize that all educational practices are built upon assumptions rooted in philosophy, and that different philosophic starting points may lead to varying educational practices.

## Idealism

### Background

Idealism is a philosophic position that has had a great deal of influence upon education down through the ages. As an educational philosophy, idealism has had less direct influence in the twentieth century than previously. Indirectly, however, its ideas still permeate Western educational thought.

William E. Hocking, a modern idealist, has pointed out that the term "idea-ism" would be a better title than "idealism."[1] This is true because idealism is more concerned with "eternal"

---

[1] William Ernest Hocking, *Types of Philosophy*, 3d ed. (New York: Charles Scribner's Sons, 1959), p. 152.

concepts (ideas), such as "truth," "beauty," and "honor," than with the high-minded striving for excellence which is referred to when we say: "She is very idealistic."

Idealism, at its core, is an emphasis on the reality of ideas, thoughts, minds, or selves, rather than a stress on material objects and forces. Idealism emphasizes mind as being basic or prior to matter, and even contends that mind is real, while matter is a by-product of mind.[2] This is in direct contrast to materialism, which claims that matter is real and mind is an accompanying phenomenon.

Historically, idealism was clearly formulated by Plato (427-347 B.C.). Athens, during Plato's lifetime, was in a state of transition. The Persian Wars had thrust Athens into a new era. Following the wars, trade and commerce grew rapidly, and foreigners settled within her walls in large numbers to take advantage of the opportunities for acquiring wealth. This greater exposure of Athens to the outside world brought new ideas into all areas of Athenian culture. These new ideas, in turn, led people to question traditional knowledge and values. At this time, also, a new group of teachers, the Sophists, arose. The teachings of the Sophists introduced controversial ideas into the fields of politics and ethics. The Sophists focused upon individualism as they sought to prepare people for the new opportunities of a more commercial society. Their emphasis on individualism was a shift from the communal culture of the past, and it led to relativism in such areas as belief and value.

Plato's philosophy can, to a large extent, be seen as a reaction to the state of flux that had destroyed the old Athenian culture. Plato's quest was a search for certain truth. He defined truth as that which is perfect and eternal. It is evident that the world of daily existence is constantly changing. Truth, therefore, could not

---

[2] In this discussion of idealism the reader should note that even though there are many types of idealism, they all have a common emphasis on ideas and mind. The following pages will build upon the implications of this central position and will not seek to deal with variations within the idealistic approach to basic philosophic and educational issues. This level of treatment will serve the purposes of this introductory text. What has been said in regard to this simplified approach to idealism will also hold true for the other philosophies studied.

be found in the imperfect and transitory world of matter. Plato believed that there were universal truths upon which all people could agree. Such truths were found in mathematics. For example, $5 + 7 = 12$ has always been true (it is an *a priori* truth), is true now, and will always be true in the future. It was Plato's contention that universal truths exist in every realm, including politics, religion, ethics, and education. To arrive at universal truths, Plato moved beyond the ever-changing world of sensory data to the world of ideas.

Idealism, with its stress on unchanging universal Truth, has had a powerful impact upon philosophical thought. The Christian church grew up in a world permeated by Neoplatonism and early amalgamated idealism with its theology. This union was most clearly set forth by Augustine (354-430) in the fifth century. Idealism has been developed in modern thought by such philosophers as René Descartes (1596-1650), George Berkeley (1685-1753), Immanuel Kant (1724-1804), and Georg Wilhelm Friedrick Hegel (1770-1831). Perhaps the most influential American educational idealist was William T. Harris (1835-1909), who founded the *Journal of Speculative Philosophy*, served as the dynamic superintendent of the Saint Louis schools during the 1870s, and later became the United States Commissioner of Education. Two twentieth-century idealists who have sought to apply idealism to modern education are J. Donald Butler and Herman H. Horne.[3] Throughout its history, idealism, has been closely linked with religion, since they both focus on the spiritual and otherworldly aspects of reality.

## Philosophic Position of Idealism

*A reality of the mind.* Perhaps the easiest way to arrive at an understanding of idealist metaphysics is to go to the most

---

[3] J. Donald Butler, *Idealism in Education* (New York: Harper & Row, 1966); Herman Harrell Horne, *The Democratic Philosophy of Education* (New York: The Macmillan Co., 1932).

influential of all idealists—Plato. Plato gives us a view of the idealist's concept of reality in his Allegory of the Cave.[4] Imagine, suggests Plato, a group of people in a dark cave, chained in such a way that they can see only the back wall of the cave. They cannot turn their heads or bodies to the right or left. Behind these chained beings is a fire, and between them and the fire is a raised pathway. Objects move along the pathway, and their shadows are cast upon the wall. The chained individuals cannot see the fire or the objects; they see only the shadows. If, questions Plato, they had been chained in this manner all their lives, would not they consider the shadows to be real in the fullest sense of the word?

Now, continues Plato, imagine that these individuals are unchained and are able to turn around and see the fire and the objects on the pathway. They would then have to readjust their conception of reality to fit the new perceptual data. Then, after having adjusted to a three-dimensional reality, they are led from the cave into the brilliance of the sunlit world. Would they not be dumbfounded by this fuller view of reality? Would they not also, in bewilderment, desire to return to the more manageable environment of the cave?

Plato's allegory suggests that the majority of humanity lives in the world of the senses—the cave. But to Plato this is not the world of ultimate reality; it is only a world of shadows and images of the "real" world. The more genuinely real world is a world of pure ideas that is beyond the world of the senses. One comes into contact with the ultimately real world through the intellect. The understanding of reality is a rare gift that is possessed by only a few people. These people (the thinkers and philosophers), therefore, should fill the most important posts in society if the social order is to be just. By way of contrast, the majority of mankind live by their senses and are not in contact with reality. They maintain a definitely inferior existence.

In summary, it might be re-emphasized that reality for the idealist is dichotomous—there is the world of the apparent,

---

4 Plato *Republic* 7. 514-17.

43

which we perceive through our senses, and the world of reality, which we perceive through our minds. The world of the mind focuses on ideas, and these eternal ideas precede and are more important than the physical world of sensation. That ideas precede material objects can be illustrated, claim the idealists, by the construction of a chair. They point out that someone had to have the idea of a chair in mind before he or she could build one to sit on. The metaphysics of idealism might be defined as a world of mind.

*Truth as ideas.* The clue to understanding the idealists' epistemology lies in their metaphysics. Since they emphasize the reality of ideas and mind, we find their theory of knowing to be principally an enterprise of mentally grasping ideas and concepts. Knowing reality is not an experience of seeing, hearing, or touching; it is rather taking hold of the idea of something and retaining it in the mind.

Truth to the idealist lies in the realm of ideas. Some idealists have postulated an Absolute Mind or Absolute Self who is constantly thinking these ideas. George Berkeley, a Christian idealist, identified the concept of the Absolute Self with God. Down through history many religious thinkers have made that same identification.

Key words in idealistic epistemology are "consistence" and "coherence." Idealists are concerned with developing a system of truth that has internal and logical consistency. We know that something is true, they claim, when it fits into the harmonious nature of the universe. Those things which are inconsistent with the ideal structure of the universe must be rejected as false. Frederick Neff has noted that

> idealism is essentially a metaphysics, and even its epistemology is metaphysical in the sense that it attempts to rationalize and justify what is metaphysically true rather than to utilize experience and methods of knowledge as a basis for the formulation of truth.[5]

[5] Frederick C. Neff, *Philosophy and American Education* (New York: The Center for Applied Research in Education, 1966), p. 36.

Truth for idealists is inherent in the very nature of the universe; and therefore it is prior to, and largely independent of, experience. Hence, the means by which ultimate knowledge is gained is not empirical. Idealists of various strains rely heavily upon intuition, revelation, and rationalism in gaining and extending knowledge. These methods are those best able to handle truth as ideas, which is the basic epistemological stance of idealism.

*Values from the ideal world.* The axiology of idealism is firmly rooted in its metaphysical outlook. If ultimate reality lies beyond this world, and if there is an Absolute Self who is the prototype of mind, then the cosmos can be thought of in terms of macrocosm and microcosm. From this viewpoint, the macrocosm can be thought of as the world of the Absolute Mind, while this earth and its sensory experiences may be thought of in terms of microcosm—a shadow of that which is ultimately real. In such a conception, it should be evident that both ethical and aesthetical criteria of goodness and beauty would be external to mankind, would be inherent in the very nature of true reality, and would be based on fixed and eternal principles.

For the idealist, the ethical life can be thought of as a life lived in harmony with the universe. If the Absolute Self is seen in terms of macrocosm, then the individual human self can be identified as a microcosmic self. In this case, the role of the individual self would be to become as much like the Absolute Self as possible. If the Absolute is viewed as the final and most ethical of all things and persons, or as God who is by definition perfect and is thus perfect in morals, the idealist epitome of ethical conduct would lie in the imitation of the Absolute Self. Humanity is moral when it is in accord with the Universal Moral Law, which is an expression of the character of the Absolute Being. A problem arises in discovering the Moral Law. That problem is not difficult for religious idealists, who accept revelation as a source of authority. On the other hand, this discovery does pose a problem for the idealist with a secular orientation. Kant's categorical imperative[6] may be viewed as one means of arriving at the Moral Law by means other than revelation.

The aesthetics of the idealist can also be seen in terms of macrocosm and microcosm. The idealist sees as beautiful the approximation or reflection of the ideal. That art which attempts to express the Absolute is categorized as aesthetically pleasing. Artists seek to capture the ultimate and universal aspects in their work. The function of art forms is not to portray literally the world to our sensibilities, but to depict the world as the Absolute Self sees it. Art is an attempt to capture reality in its perfect form. From this viewpoint, photography would not be considered a true art form, since its business is to depict things the way they happen to be in our experience. Art from the idealist's point of view can be thought of as the idealization of sensory perceptions.

## Idealism and Education

In terms of the idealist metaphor, the learner can be viewed as a microcosmic self who is in the process of becoming more like the Absolute Self. In one sense, the individual self is an extension of the Absolute Self and, as such, has the same attributes in their undeveloped form. Motivationally the idealist pupil "is characterized by . . . the will to perfection. Whatever he does, he does as well as he can. . . . He strives for perfection because the ideal person is perfect."[7]

In a universe whose reality is centered in idea and mind, the most important aspect of learners is their intellect; they are microcosmic minds. It is at the level of mind that the educational endeavor must be primarily aimed, since true knowledge can be gained only through the mind. From this perspective, Plato proclaimed that in the best of all worlds the rulers would be philosophers. Why? Because only they had dealt with the world of

[6] Act only on that maxim which will enable you at the same time to will that it be a universal law.

[7] Herman Harrell Horne, "An Idealistic Philosophy of Education," in *Philosophies of Education*, National Society for the Study of Education, Forty-first Yearbook, Part I (Chicago: University of Chicago Press, 1942), pp. 156-57.

ultimate reality which lies beyond this sensory world. Due to their philosophic view, idealists concentrate on the mental development of the learner.

In an idealist school, teachers have a crucial position. It is the teachers who serve the students as living examples of what they can become. Teachers stand closer to the Absolute than do the students, because they have more knowledge about the ultimate world of the mind. They know more about "reality" and are thus able to act as intermediaries between the microcosmic self of the learner and the macrocosmic Absolute Self. The teachers' role is to pass on knowledge of reality and to be examples of the ethical ideal. They are patterns for the students to follow in both their intellectual and social lives.

The subject matter of idealism is viewed in terms of its epistemological position. If truth is ideas, then the curriculum must be formed around those subjects that bring students into contact with ideas. The idealist curriculum emphasizes, therefore, the study of the humanities. For many idealists the proper study of mankind is humanity. History and the study of literature are found at the center of their curricular systems, because these subjects help students most in their search for the ideal humanity and ideal society. Pure mathematics is also an appropriate discipline, since it is based upon universal *a priori* principles and it provides methods for dealing with abstractions.

Words, either written or spoken, form the basis of idealism's method of instruction, because it is through words that ideas move from one mind to another. The aim of this method might be defined as the absorption of ideas. The library tends to be the center of educational activity in the idealist school. It is in the library that students come into contact with the significant ideas of mankind. The classroom, in one sense, may be seen as an operating arm or extension of the library—a place in which books and ideas still form the center of attention. Teacher methodology in the classroom is often seen in terms of lecturing in a context in which knowledge is being transferred from the teacher to the student. Teachers are also apt to initiate discussions through which they and their students handle the ideas of readings and lectures as they bring concepts into sharper focus.

47

The idealist teacher would not be especially excited about a field trip to the local dairy or the teaching of auto mechanics in high school, because such activities lie at the periphery of life's true meaning—they deal more with the shadowy sensory world than with ultimate reality. They are not, therefore, proper "educational" activities.[8]

Detractors of idealism have pointed to this type of education as an ivory-tower experience. That criticism does not bother the idealists, who claim that the real purpose of schools and universities is to provide a place where the mind can "think" and "know" without being bothered by the transitory experiences of everyday life.[9]

It should come as no surprise that idealism, with its stress on the ideas of the past (especially those ideas dealing with the Absolute), has a conservative social impact. For idealism, the changeless world of Ultimate Reality is of a higher order than the transitory world of the senses. Mankind, when it has finally come into contact with the unchanging ideas of reality, must order its life to fit into the context of that reality. The social function of the school, for the idealist, is to preserve the heritage and to pass on the knowledge of the past. The school is not an agent of change. It is rather a sustainer of the *status quo*.

[8] Following from Plato's aristocratic notions of society and education, idealists have tended to view formal education as being for the select few rather than for the masses. Plato divided people into three basic levels, according to whether they lived by their appetites, passions, or intellects. The type of education that most idealists have been concerned with is for those who are chiefly governed by their intellects. Those outside the intellectual elite should receive vocational and technical studies. For people in the latter group, instruction in the world of things (through either apprenticeship or vocational schooling) would be appropriate, since this harmonizes with their needs and the cast of their minds—minds unable to transcend the world of shadows.

[9] Van Cleve Morris, *Philosophy and the American School*, p. 183.

# Realism

## Background

Realism, to a certain extent, is a reaction against the abstractness and otherworldliness of idealism. The basic starting point for the realist is that the objects of our senses exist in their own right quite independently of their being known by a mind. The fundamental difference between realism and idealism might be illustrated by the example of a tree on a deserted island. The idealist would say that such a tree exists only if it is in some mind (including the mind of a transcendent being) or if there is knowledge of it. The realist, on the other hand, holds that whether or not anyone or anything is thinking about the tree, it nevertheless exists—matter is independent of mind.

Well-defined realism finds its genesis in Plato's pupil, Aristotle (384-322 B.C.). On the one hand, Aristotle was deeply influenced by Plato; but, on the other hand, his thinking showed a definite divergence from Platonic idealism. Aristotle held that the basic constituents of every object were form and matter. Form may be equated with Plato's conception of idea, while matter can be thought of in terms of the material making up any particular sensory object. According to Aristotle, form can exist without matter (e. g., the idea of God or the idea of dog), but there can be no matter without form. Aristotle did not downplay the importance of form or ideas. His radical departure from his teacher came with the belief that a better understanding of universal ideas could be obtained through the study of particular things or matter.

It was Aristotle's focus on the possibility of arriving at conceptions of universal form through the study of material objects that led him to lay the basic structure for what has evolved into the modern physical, life, and social sciences. Aristotle was a great organizer and categorizer. Even the beginning college student has probably seen Aristotle's name in the history of such diverse fields as physics, botany, zoology, sociology, psychology, logic, and the various aspects of formal philosophy. In Aristotle people found the rationale upon which they have developed the modern sciences.

Realism found its way into the modern world largely through the influence of Francis Bacon's (1561-1626) inductive methodology (the scientific method) and John Locke's (1632-1704) proposal that the human mind is a blank sheet (*tabula rasa*) that receives impressions from the environment. Perhaps Harry S. Broudy has made as strong an argument as anyone for realism in modern education.[10]

## Philosophic Position of Realism

*A reality of things.* For the realist, ultimate reality is not in the realm of the mind. The universe is composed of matter in motion, so it is the physical world in which mankind lives that makes up reality. This is a straightforward approach to a world of things that operate according to laws which are built into the very fabric of the universe. The vast cosmos rolls on despite mankind and its knowledge.

The universe is not unlike a giant machine in which humanity is both spectator and participant. The laws controlling the cosmos not only govern the physical universe, but they are also operating in the moral, psychological, social, political, and economic spheres. In other words, the realist sees reality in terms of things that operate according to natural law. In its variation of configurations, realism is found at the philosophic base of much modern science.

*Truth through observation.* The epistemology of realism is a common-sense approach to the world that bases its method upon sensory perception. W. E. Hocking notes that "realism as a general temper of mind is a disposition to keep ourselves and our preferences out of our judgment of things, letting the objects speak for themselves."[11]

[10] Harry S. Broudy, *Building a Philosophy of Education*, 2d ed. (Englewood Cliffs, N.J.: Prentice Hall, 1961.

[11] Hocking, *Types of Philosophy*, p. 225. Cf. Titus and Smith, *Living Issues in Philosophy*, p. 451.

Truth, for the realist, is viewed as observable fact. Sense perception is the medium for gaining knowledge. Realism utilizes the inductive method in investigating the natural world and in arriving at general principles from observations. The realist seeks to discover how the world works by examining it. The natural law thereby discovered is believed to be built into the nature of reality. It may be thought of as being absolute, prior to mankind's experience with it, and unchangeable. "The world," write Titus and Smith, "is what it is, no matter what men think about it."[12]

From that perspective, the existence of "Natural Law" for the realist may be viewed as having much the same magnitude as Absolute Mind for the idealist. Both positions are conceptions of the ultimate and "out-there" nature of truth and reality. Realism turns to the correspondence theory for validating its conception of truth (i.e., truth is that which conforms to the actual situation as perceived by the observer).

*Values from nature.* According to the realist, values are also obtained by the observation of nature. Through a study of the natural order, one comes to know the laws that provide the basis for ethical and aesthetic judgment. Values derived from this source are permanent, since they are rooted in a universe that is stable—even though, from the human point of view, it is being more fully understood all the time.

The ethical basis of realism might be viewed as the law of nature. Nature, claims the realist, has a moral law. All people have that law or at least have the possibility of discovering it. Just as gravity is a universal law in the physical world, so are supply and demand a law in the economic realm. It was with this concept of moral law in mind that Thomas Jefferson referred to the "inalienable rights" of man. Humanity must look to nature for a clearer definition of these rights.

---

[12]Ibid., p. 449. It should be noted that the New Realists and the Critical Realists differ over whether the mind perceives the object itself or a representation of that object. That difference, however, is not of major importance for the level of argument being followed in this presentation.

Nature also contains the criteria for beauty. A beautiful art form, from the viewpoint of realism, reflects the logic and order of the universe. In one sense it is "re-presenting," or presenting anew, the rationality of nature as that rationality is revealed in pattern, balance, line, and form. In painting, the objective of artists should be to recreate what they perceive as realistically as possible. From this perspective, photography definitely qualifies as an art form.

## Realism and Education[13]

To the realist, students are viewed as functioning organisms that can, through sensory experience, perceive the natural order of the world and thereby come into contact with "reality." Pupils can see, feel, and taste. The world is a "thing," and pupils can know the world through their senses.

Many realists view students as persons who are subject to natural law and are therefore not free in their choices. Students, claim these exponents of realism, respond to environmental stimuli. It is not uncommon to find realists advocating a behavioristic psychology. At its most extreme form, this approach sees students as part of the great universal machine. Such students can be programmed in a manner similar to the way computers are programmed. Of course, such programming may not at first be successful. In that case, students must be reinforced, disciplined, and shaped until they have learned to make the proper responses.

If the student is thought of as a spectator viewing the universal machine, then the teacher can be seen as a more sophisticated observer who knows a great deal about the laws of the cosmos. The role of the teacher, therefore, is to give accurate information about reality to the student in the quickest and most efficient manner. For this reason the teacher's own biases and personality should be as muted as possible. The function of teaching is to demonstrate the regularities and laws of nature and to pass on to

[13] A systematic approach to this topic is found in Wm. Oliver Martin, *Realism in Education* (New York: Harper & Row, 1969).

the student those facts of the natural world that have been verified by research.

In harmony with its metaphysical and epistemological perspective, the curriculum in the realist school emphasizes the subject matter of the physical world taught in such a way that the orderliness underlying the universe is evident. The sciences stand at the center of the realist curriculum, since the laws of nature are best understood through the subject matter of nature. Mathematics also finds a central place in realist curricular thinking, since mathematics is an example of the highest form of order. Mathematics is a precise, abstract, symbolic system for describing the laws of the universe.

The realist's conception of the universe, with its emphasis on statistical and quantitative studies, has largely shaped much of our knowledge of the social sciences. The realist views the curriculum in terms of knowledge which can be measured. Many realists have taken for their credo the position espoused by Edward L. Thorndike in 1918 when he remarked: "Whatever exists at all exists in some amount. To know it thoroughly involves its quantity as well as its quality."[14] Thus the focus of the realist curriculum is on demonstrable facts and the structural frameworks of the academic disciplines that give meaning to those facts.[15] The "symbolics of information" (language and mathematics) are also important in the curriculum, because they provide "the entrance to an academic discipline" as well as an encoded system for passing on accumulated knowledge.[16]

The instructional method of the realists is closely related to their epistemology. If truth is gained through sensory perception, then learning experiences should be organized, to a large extent,

---

[14] Edward L. Thorndike, "The Nature, Purposes, and General Methods of Measurements of Educational Products," in *The Measurement of Educational Products*, National Society for the Study of Education, Seventeenth Yearbook, Part II (Bloomington, Ill.: Public School Publishing Co., 1918), pp. 16-17.

[15] Gerald L. Gutek, *Philosophical and Ideological Perspectives on Education* (Englewood Cliffs, New Jersey: Prentice Hall, 1988), pp. 46-49.

[16] Harry S. Broudy, *The Uses of Schooling* (New York: Routledge, 1988), p. 81; Harry S. Broudy, "What Schools Should and Should Not Teach," *Peabody Journal of Education*, October, 1976, p. 36.

in a manner that utilizes the senses. It was from this perspective that Comenius, the seventeenth-century Moravian bishop and educator, became famous for his *Orbis Pictus*, in which he astonished the educational world by suggesting that visual aids—pictures—be used in instructing the young in Latin vocabulary. In the late eighteenth and early nineteenth centuries Pestalozzi took the realist method a giant step forward when he called for the use of physical object lessons in the classroom, since students would learn best if they could feel, smell, and hear an object as well as see it.

The modern realist favors demonstrations in the classroom, field trips, and the use of audio-visual aids in situations where field trips would not be practical or would be too time-consuming. This does not mean that the realist denies the validity of symbolic knowledge (as found in books). It rather implies that the symbol has no existential status, but is viewed simply as a means of representing or communicating about the real world.

The method of realists involves teaching for the mastery of facts in order to develop an understanding of natural law. They are concerned that the students comprehend the basic laws of nature. In this approach they rely heavily on inductive logic as they move from the particular facts of sensory experience to the more general laws inferable from this data.

The mechanistic world view of many realists also leads them to favor teaching machines and programmed learning. Through a machine a great deal of accurate information about the world may be passed to the student quickly and efficiently. The whole concept of teaching machines is compatible with the idea that people are machines and can be programmed. From this perspective, teaching is best when it is most objective and dehumanized, since humans are a source of error.

It should be apparent that the social position of the school in realism closely approximates that of the school in idealism. The purpose of the school is to transmit knowledge that has been settled upon by those who have a clear concept of empirical science and natural law and its function in the universe. The realist school focuses on the conservation of the heritage—it is concerned with passing on the proven facts and the structural frameworks that provide meaning for those facts.

# Neo-scholasticism

## Background

Scholasticism was an intellectual movement that developed in western Europe between 1050 and 1350. This movement at first found its home in the monastic orders, but as universities arose in the thirteenth century, it came to dominate their curricula. Scholastic scholars were not as interested in seeking new truth as they were in proving existing truth through rational processes.

A major event that stimulated the rise of scholasticism was the emergence of Aristotle's writings in Christian Europe. Most of his writings had been lost to the Christian world during the Middle Ages. They had, however, been preserved in the Islamic world beyond the pale of medieval Christendom. Those of Aristotle's writings and ideas that had been available to Christian Europe had been largely neglected. Medieval theology and philosophy had been founded upon the Augustinian synthesis of Platonic and early Christian thought. In the twelfth century, however, translations of Aristotle and Arabic and Jewish commentaries on his works began to appear in western Europe. These new ideas were not always in harmony with accepted Christian thought, and Aristotelian philosophy turned out to be just as divisive to medieval Christendom as Darwinism would later be to nineteenth-century Christianity. It soon became apparent that these two bodies of knowledge, medieval Christianity and Aristotelianism, had to be harmonized. The scholastics sought to organize the data of revelation systematically by the use of Aristotelian deductive logic and to harmonize the ideas of revelation with the philosophy of Aristotle. In essence, scholasticism can be seen as the attempt to rationalize theology in order to buttress faith by reason.

Thomas Aquinas (1225-1274) was the foremost scholar in this crisis. The results of his work have been preserved in his *Summa*

*Theologica.* The basic approach developed by Aquinas was that a person should acquire as much knowledge as possible through the use of human reason and then rely on faith in that realm beyond the scope of human understanding. The philosophy of Aquinas (Thomism) is currently accepted as the official philosophic position of the Roman Catholic Church.

The essence of scholasticism is rationalism. Neo-scholasticism is a new or updated form of scholasticism with its emphasis on, and appeal to, human reason. Neo-scholasticism is therefore a modern statement of a traditional philosophy.

In twentieth-century educational thought, neo-scholasticism is a philosophical position that has two branches. The most important segment, in terms of educational establishments, is the religious branch, which forms the substructure of Roman Catholic educational philosophy. In the literature this segment is often referred to as "scholastic realism," "religious realism," and "ecclesiastical neo-Thomism." Jacques Maritain is a leading advocate of religious neo-scholasticism. The second division, the secular branch, is represented by such men as Mortimer J. Adler and Robert M. Hutchins.[17] Their beliefs are often labeled "rational humanism," "classical realism," and "secular neo-Thomism." The basic educational ideas of these groups find a united expression for their rationale in the theory of perennialism, which will be discussed in chapter V.

## Philosophic Position of Neo-scholasticism

*A reality of reason (and God).* As noted above, there are some differences of opinion among philosophers over the labeling of the neo-scholastics. This is due partly to the fact that neo-scholasticism overlaps other philosophic positions and partly to the fact that it has two distinct roots. The first of these roots is

[17] Jacques Maritain, *Education at the Crossroads* (New Haven, Conn.: Yale University Press, 1943); Mortimer J. Adler, "In Defense of the Philosophy of Education," in *Philosophies of Education*, National Society for the Study of Education, Forty-first Yearbook, Part I (Chicago: University of Chicago Press, 1942), pp. 197-249; Robert M. Hutchins, *The Higher Learning In America* (New Haven, Conn.: Yale University Press, 1936).

Aristotle, who laid the foundations of realism. The second root is Aquinas, who synthesized Aristotelian philosophy and Christianity.

Aristotle laid the groundwork of neo-scholasticism through his conception of man as a rational animal and his development of deductive logic. For Aristotle, the most important question people can ask about things is their purpose. He held that since humans are the only creatures endowed with the ability to think, mankind's highest purpose is to use that ability. Aristotle also taught that the universe has design and order, and that every result has a cause. The design, order, and cause-and-effect relationships in the world, he claimed, point to a First Cause or an Unmoved Mover. Aquinas equated Aristotle's Unmoved Mover with the Christian God. God, Aquinas suggested, is pure reason; and the universe He created is therefore also reason. Humans, as rational animals, live in a rational world that they are capable of understanding.

The metaphysics of the neo-scholastics is a two-sided coin. On the one side is the natural world that is open to reason. On the other side is the supernatural realm, which is understood through intuition, revelation, and faith. Scientists deal with the natural aspect, but the spiritual side is beyond their reach. Neo-scholastics hold the nature of the universe to be permanent and unchanging.

*Truth through rationalism (and inspiration).* If, as the neo-scholastics claim, the rational human mind is naturally oriented toward the rationality of the universe, then it follows that the mind can take hold of certain truths by itself—it can intuit truth. Intuitive or self-evident truths, postulate the neo-scholastics, are found in analytic statements. An analytic statement is a statement that contains its predicate in its subject. Examples of analytic statements are "God is good" and "Two things equal to the same thing are equal to each other." These kinds of statements, in which the predicate is analyzed out of the subject, do not have to be tested in experience. One does not need to draw two lines equal to a third and then measure them to see if they are equal. The intellect reveals that this is true—it is self-evident and has been intuited as true.

A second form of truth for the neo-scholastic is found in synthetic statements. Synthetic truth depends upon our experience. An example of a synthetic statement is "San Francisco is 3,224 miles from New York." Synthetic statements lie in the realm of science and empirical experience. They must be tested, since their predicate is not contained in their subject. On the other hand, analytic statements are logically and intrinsically true.

Neo-scholastics hold, in contrast to empiricists, that analytic statements form first principles and are therefore of a higher order than synthetic statements. These self-evident statements open up a whole realm of truth to the neo-scholastic that cannot be reached by science. For the secular neo-scholastic, truth can be known through reason and intuition. The religious branch of this philosophic approach adds supernatural revelation as a source of knowledge that can put finite humans in contact with the mind of God.

Both branches of neo-scholasticism rely heavily upon reason and the deductive forms of Aristotelian logic. Induction is not rejected, however, since information gained through the senses forms a part of the raw material used in deductive thinking.

In summary, it should be noted that the neo-scholastics believe in a hierarchy of truth. At the lower level people rely on reason. This is the realm of nature and science and is quite limited. The higher level is the realm of first principles and faith. These two realms often overlap, and thus they form two routes to the same truth. For example, the existence of God is a matter of faith, even though Aquinas posited five logical proofs of God's existence in his *Summa Theologica*. The neo-scholastic values most highly those truths that are logical, permanent, and unchanging.

*Values related to rationality.* It has been noted that reason is the central pillar in both neo-scholastic metaphysics and epistemology. This is also true of their ethics. The moral life is the life that is in harmony with reason. Humans are basically rational beings, and the good act is controlled by rationality. People sometimes are controlled and led astray by their wills, desires, and emotions. Good people, however, are the ones whose desires and wills are subservient to their intellects; if they know what is right, they will do it, because it is reasonable to do what is good. The ethics of neo-scholasticism might be seen in terms of acting rationally.

Aesthetic theory is not as clear-cut in the neo-scholastic school of philosophy as in other philosophies. This may be due to the fact that their heavy stress on the rational nature of mankind is antithetical to the faculties of will and emotion which we generally associate with art forms. Van Cleve Morris, after noting the inborn tendency of mankind to creativity, has summed up the neo-scholastic approach to art as "'creative intuition,' a somewhat mystical, probing lurch of the intellect beyond itself," as if the art were seeking to escape from reason—as in the case of modern art and poetry.[18] This is a concept built upon the desire of people to give to their material the meaning that is, in Aristotelian terms, potentially already in it. Art, therefore, is self-evident to artists. They intuit meaning to art rather than approaching it logically, even though they may appreciate a work of art through the pleasure it gives the intellect.

## Neo-scholasticism and Education

Both branches of neo-scholasticism are consistent in the relationship between their philosophic stance and their educational recommendations. The student, for both groups, is a rational being who has a natural potential to acquire Truth and knowledge. Religious neo-scholastics also see the learner as a spiritual being who may relate to God. The responsibility of the school is to help the student develop these capacities.

Faculty psychology is the perspective from which the rational powers of the learner are viewed by the neo-scholastics. In this view, the mind is thought to have different potentials, or faculties, which must be carefully developed. Therefore, the faculty of reason is trained through the formal discipline inherent in the study of those subjects having the most logical organization, the faculty of memory is developed by having students memorize, and the faculty of the will is strengthened by having

---

[18] Van Cleve Morris, *Philosophy and the American School*, pp. 266-67.

students engage in tasks that require a high degree of perseverance for completion. Through such procedures, the faculties are developed and the will is brought under submission to reason.

Teachers in a neo-scholastic frame of reference are viewed as mental disciplinarians with the capability of developing reason, memory, and will power in their students. Initiative in education, claims the neo-scholastic (in agreement with idealists and realists), lies with the teacher. It is the teacher's responsibility, in conjunction with other educational authorities, to decide what knowledge the child should learn. It is helpful if this decision harmonizes with the child's interest and curiosity; but subject matter concerns, rather than student desires, are central to the educational endeavor. Intelligence demands the discipline of developing an understanding of those aspects of reality that are permanent and unalterable.

The ecclesiastical neo-scholastic sees the role of teachers to be that of spiritual leaders as well as mental disciplinarians. Teachers lead the child not only through the realm of reason, but also through the more important sphere of faith.

Secular neo-scholastics insist that, since humans are rational beings, the curriculum should give priority to the cultivation of the rational aspects of mankind. The mind, therefore, must be trained to think, and education should focus on sharpening the intellect, so that people will be able to understand the Absolute Truth of the cosmos. The mind must be strengthened and toughened if it is to reach that Truth.

From this perspective, it is felt by neo-scholastics that those subject matters having internal logic are best able to achieve the aim of education and should therefore be at the center of the curriculum. Mathematics is seen by many secular neo-scholastics as the nearest approach mankind has made to Pure Reason. Mathematics is uncontaminated by the irregularities of the ordinary affairs of humanity and therefore most nearly approximates the rational nature of the universe. Of somewhat less precision, but of great importance in strengthening the mind, are foreign languages—especially those that are most rigorously systematic. Thus Latin and Greek have often stood at the top of the recommended linguistic studies, while the less regular modern languages are lower in the hierarchy. Other topics of study considered especially important are logic and the works of the great minds of the past. The religious branch of neo-scholasticism is in basic agreement with its secular relative, but would hasten to include the systematic study of dogma and doctrine as subjects of primary importance.

The subject matter of the neo-scholastic tradition has two functions: (1) to explain the world to the student and (2) to train the intellect to understand that world. Their curricular stress is upon those subjects that emphasize the intellectual and spiritual aspects of culture.

Neo-scholastic methodology generally focuses on training the intellectual powers. This approach is rooted in the concept of mental discipline. The intellect is strengthened through exercises in reason and memory in relation to the discipline inherent in the subject matter. This training of the intellect has been likened by some to mental calisthenics. The idea runs parallel to building up the physical body. Just as the corporeal muscles are developed through rigorous exercise, so the mind is strengthened by strenuous mental exertion. The training of the will to accept the idea of performing naturally demanding tasks is a by-product of the methodology.

Like other traditional philosophies, neo-scholasticism has a conservative social function. In the eyes of many it is a regressive social philosophy that faces modern social problems on the basis of thirteenth-century thought patterns.

## Perspective

Despite their differing viewpoints, the traditional philosophies have certain characteristics in common. Each has metaphysics as its primary concern, each holds that the universe contains truth of an *a priori* and objective sort that is awaiting discovery by mankind, and each believes that both truth and value are eternal and unchanging rather than relative and transient.

In education the traditional philosophies also have likenesses as well as differences. For example, each sees the teacher as an authoritative person who knows what the student needs to learn; each has set forth a curriculum based on its version of the "solid" subjects that are "heavy" in intellectual content; and each views education and schooling in a conservative vein, since their function is to transfer the heritage of the past to the present generation.

All of these philosophies have made an impact upon twentieth-century education. Certainly the traditional bookishness and intellectualism of Western education have been heavily influenced by idealist and neo-scholastic presuppositions. One of the interesting chapters in the history of education has been the struggle of realism against an entrenched idealism and neo-scholasticism as realistic educators and philosophers sought to make room in educational institutions for sensory experience and the sciences. This struggle began in the eighteenth-century Enlightenment, and the final victory was not achieved until the twentieth century. The influence of Darwinism aided realism in a powerful manner in the final phases of this struggle. It will be seen in chapter V that the impact of the traditional philosophies on twentieth-century education is largely felt through the influence of essentialism, perennialism, and behaviorism.

Chapter IV turns from traditional philosophies to modern philosophies. The modern philosophies approach the basic issues of life from a different perspective than the traditional ones, and their answers will provide a broader base from which individuals can begin to develop personal philosophies.

# MODERN PHILOSOPHIES AND EDUCATION 4

Chapter III surveyed the relationship between education and the traditional philosophies of idealism, realism, and neo-scholasticism. It was noted that different philosophic positions lead to variations in educational emphases and practices. This chapter will continue examining that relationship in terms of the modern philosophic stances of pragmatism and existentialism.

Traditional philosophies had a basic similarity in the fact that they were primarily concerned with metaphysics—the issue of reality. With the modern philosophies there has been a definite shift in the hierarchical importance of the three basic philosophic categories. This shift was stimulated by the findings of modern science. For centuries the knowledge and philosophic perspective of mankind had remained fairly stable. What new knowledge was discovered was generally not of such a quantity or quality that societies had difficulty fitting it into their world view and daily practice. That stability, however, began to change in the seventeenth and eighteenth centuries. First came the new scientific discoveries and theories. They were soon followed by technological breakthroughs that made the industrial revolution possible and brought disruption and major discontinuities to the traditional social and philosophic patterns of the Western world. Throughout the nineteenth and twentieth centuries these advances in scientific knowledge, with their corresponding effects upon society, have continued to accelerate; and, as a result, many people came to reject an absolute reality that is static or even one that can be known. From the human point of view, it seems to many people that truth, as well as mankind's knowledge of truth, is relative and that there are no universal certainties. That conclusion has led the modern philosophies to avoid the issue of ultimate reality and to focus on relativist approaches to truth and value from the perspective of social groups (pragmatism) and from the viewpoint of individualism (existentialism).

In the shift from metaphysics, pragmatism has seen epistemology as the central philosophic issue, while existentialism has moved the focus of priority to axiology. It will be seen that this shift in philosophic interest has led to major alterations in educational ideas concerning the nature of the student, the role of the teacher, the content emphasis of the curriculum, the preferred methods of instruction, and the social function of education and the school.

## Pragmatism

### Background

Pragmatism is America's contribution to the history of philosophical thought. It has come to prominence during the past one hundred years and is associated with such names as Charles S. Peirce (1839-1914), William James (1842-1910), and John Dewey (1859-1952).

Traditional philosophies were static and tended to account for things as they were. They were sufficient in societies that experienced very little change. The last half of the nineteenth century, however, saw unprecedented change as the industrial revolution reached high gear. Industrialism, urbanization, and mass migrations of populations were central factors on the American scene. Change appeared to be a central feature of human existence. The intellectual arena saw the development and wide acceptance of the theories of biological and social Darwinism as people sought to rationalize and deal with the concept of change. Pragmatism (also called "experimentalism" and "instrumentalism") was the philosophic reaction to these phenomena.

William James defined pragmatism as *"the attitude of looking away from first things, principles, 'categories,' supposed necessities; and of looking towards last things, fruits, consequences, facts."*[1] Pragmatism was critical of the older systems of philosophy, which, claimed the pragmatists, made the mistake of looking for ultimates, absolutes, and eternal essences. The pragmatists emphasized empirical science, the changing world and its problems, and nature as the all-inclusive reality beyond which their faith in science would not allow them to go.

Pragmatism has intellectual antecedents in those Greek thinkers, such as Heraclitus (fifth century B.C.), who postulated the inevitability of change, and the British empiricists (seventeenth and eighteenth centuries), who maintained that people can know only what their senses experience. Pragmatic thought in education has been most influentially expressed in the writings of Dewey,[2] whose ideas have stimulated widespread experimentation in twentieth-century theory and practice.

The impact of pragmatism upon modern education has been most widely felt through the influence of the progressives. Pragmatism has also affected education, both directly and indirectly, through reconstructionism, futurism, and educational humanism. All of these theories will be discussed in chapter V.

## Philosophic Position of Pragmatism

*An experiential reality.* Some pragmatists deny that their philosophic position even has a metaphysics. That is undoubtedly due to the fact that traditional metaphysics has been concerned with an "ultimate" and "absolute" realm of reality beyond the grasp of mankind's empirical experience. The

---

[1] William James, *Pragmatism* (New York: Longmans, Green and Co., 1907), pp. 54-55.

[2] See especially, John Dewey, *Democracy and Education* (New York: The Macmillan Company, 1916); and John Dewey, *Experience and Education* (New York: The Macmillan Company, 1938).

pragmatist, on the other hand, claims that if there is such an order of reality, human beings have no way of knowing about it. From the pragmatic viewpoint, mind and matter are not two separate and independent substances. People know about matter only as they experience it and reflect upon that experience with their minds. Reality, therefore, is never divorced from the human knower.

From the pragmatist's perspective, humanity lives in what Plato described as the cave of sensory perception. This, they claim, may not be the sum total of reality; but, like it or not, the cave is all we have. We live in a world of experience and have no way of knowing whether what others claim lies beyond human experience has any truth or reality.

With the passage of time, mankind's experience changes, and therefore the pragmatists' concept of reality changes. Their metaphysical scheme allows for no absolutes, no *a priori* principles, or unchangeable natural laws. Reality is not an abstract "thing." Rather, it is a transactional experience that is constantly undergoing change. As William James put it, man lives in "a universe with the lid off." Dewey, like James, turned away from the older notions of a closed world with fixed limits and restricted possibilities. The pragmatist points out that cosmological reality has been undergoing change across time. For example, cosmic reality for many centuries centered around the geocentric theory, which placed a stationary earth at the center of the universe; then the broadened experience of Copernicus allowed the development of a heliocentric "reality"; and subsequent extensions of experience in the twentieth century led to a new view of "reality" focused upon universal relativity. Therefore, claim the pragmatists, reality is not fixed but is in a constant state of flux as humanity's experience broadens. What is "real" today may not be real tomorrow, since reality cannot be divorced from experience any more than matter may be separated from mind. We live in a dynamic universe that is undergoing a constant state of change; and such things as scientific laws, which are based upon mankind's limited experience, must be stated in terms of probability, rather than in terms of absolutes.

*Truth as what works.* Pragmatism is basically an epistemological undertaking. Knowledge, according to the pragmatist, is rooted in experience. Mankind has an active and exploratory mind, rather than one that is passive and receptive. As a result, people do not simply receive knowledge; they make it as they interact with the environment. The seeking of knowledge, therefore, is a transaction. Human beings act upon the environment and then undergo certain consequences. They learn from this transactional experience with the world around them.

The clearest and most extensive discussion of the pragmatic epistemological method for transforming experience into knowledge was given by Dewey in *How We Think* (1910). According to Dewey, the process of reflective thinking may be seen as having five steps.[3] First, individuals, as they actively move through life, meet up with a problem or a disturbing situation that temporarily inhibits their progress. This situation provides a moment of hesitation, during which the process of thought is initiated as the mind begins to focus on the problem at hand. The second step is an intellectualization of what was at first an emotional response to blocked activity. During this phase, steps are taken by the individual to diagnose the situation and to come to grips with the precise nature of the problem. The third stage involves an inventory of possible solutions. People let their minds freely suggest every conceivable potential solution to the problem. These possible solutions take the form of "guiding ideas" or hypotheses. Phase four is an exercise in reasoning as the possible solutions of the third stage are conjectured upon for their probable consequences if put into action. The mind operates in a line of thought running from cause to effect in an attempt to narrow the choices to the hypothesis that will be successful in overcoming the current difficulty. The fifth stage is concerned with testing the most reasonable hypothesis by action to see if the conjectured consequences do in fact occur. If the hypothesis or proposed answer works when applied to the world of experience, then it is

---

[3] John Dewey, How *We Think: A Restatement of the Relation of Reflective Thinking to the Educative Process,* new ed. (New York: D. C. Heath and Co., 1933), pp. 106-118.

true—truth is what works. If an hypothesis does not work or does not enable a person to overcome the problem, then it is unverified and fails to come under the pragmatic definition of truth. If an acted-upon hypothesis proves to be false, then the person must go back to at least phase four and seek truth in an alternate hypothesis.

At this point it is important to recognize that knowledge, from the pragmatic perspective, needs to be carefully distinguished from belief. The authenticity of what persons may claim to believe is a matter of private concern, but what they claim to know must be capable of demonstration to any impartial, qualified observer. In other words, beliefs are private, while knowledge is at all times regarded as public. The pragmatist notes that although some beliefs may be founded on knowledge, certainly many of them are not. From the pragmatist's viewpoint, a statement that purports to be true is one that can be phrased in "if . . . then" language and can be tested by public empirical experience.

The pragmatic epistemological position gives no place to such things as *a priori* concepts and Absolute Truths. Mankind lives in a constantly expanding and changing experiential world, and "what works" today may prove to be an insufficient explanation tomorrow. Therefore, truth is relative, and what is true today may not be true in the future or in a different situational context.

*Values from society.* The axiology of pragmatism is directly related to its epistemology. Just as humanity is ultimately responsible for truth and knowledge, so it is also responsible for values. Values are relative, and there are no absolute principles on which we can lean. As cultures change, so do values. This does not mean that morality must of necessity fluctuate from day to day, but it does mean that no axiological precept may be regarded as universally binding.

In the realm of ethics, the criterion of good conduct can be defined, from the position of the pragmatist, as the social test. That which is ethically good is that which "works." It should be noted, however, that just as the epistemological test is of a public nature, so we find that the ethical test is based on the good of society and not merely upon a private or personal good. For example, if my goal is to gain wealth, then I might assume that it would be good (it would achieve my goal) if I became a thief. In this way I would personally achieve a position of wealth. Since the results are satisfactory, in the sense that it worked to make me rich, I might be tempted to think that my thievery was moral. But, claims the pragmatist, while this may work for an individual, it could not possibly work for the entire social system, since no one would be able to accumulate wealth if everyone else was stealing it. Therefore, when put to the public test, stealing fails to work and cannot be defined as good or moral, since it makes civilized living an impossibility.

By this view of ethics the early pragmatists were able to validate the last six commandments (those dealing with relationships between people) of the Judeo-Christian Decalogue while ignoring the first four (those dealing with the relationship between mankind and God), which were impossible to test by empirical means. This was a crucial development in their approach to ethics for several reasons: (1) the ethical value system of Western civilization was based upon these moral precepts; (2) moral education had been tied to the Hebrew-Christian tradition; (3) the accepted way of teaching these morals in their religious context was being undermined by Darwinism and biblical criticism; and (4) if civilization was to have continuity, then a new foundation for morality needed to be found—one that could be taught in the public schools. The pragmatists put forth an axiological test that they believed would solve this crucial social problem.

It should not be inferred from the above discussion that the pragmatists were in favor of such things as universal commandments or moral codes. On the contrary, they advocated that the individual should learn how to make difficult moral decisions, not by falling back on rigidly prescribed principles, but by determining which course of intelligent action was likely to produce the best results in human terms. It just so happens that traditional Western values could be validated by the pragmatic method, while they were at the same time being purged of their unscientific "religious" elements, which were not amenable to

69

the public test of experience. Thus a new rationale could be developed for teaching traditional ethics in what was becoming a secular society.

Aesthetic criteria for the pragmatist are also found in human experience, as opposed to the traditional philosophies, which found their aesthetic determinants beyond the confines of experience. Dewey, in *Art As Experience*, provides the clue to the pragmatist's approach to aesthetics. The way in which aesthetic evaluation is arrived at may be called "social taste." Concepts of beauty depend upon how people feel when they have an "aesthetic" experience. If, in the presence of a given work, they see new meanings in life and have new dimensions of feeling, which enable them to make better emotional contact with their fellow beings, then they are experiencing a work of true art. From this perspective, the pragmatist would abolish the distinction between fine and practical art. Both of these traditional categories enter into the human experience and can lead to aesthetic appreciation.

## Pragmatism and Education

The important thing about students, from the pragmatists' epistemological viewpoint, is that they have experiences. They are experiencing individuals who are capable of using their intelligence to resolve problematic situations. Students learn as they act upon their environment and are, in turn, acted upon by that environment as they undergo the consequences of their actions. For the pragmatist, the school experience is a part of life, rather than a preparation for life. As such, the way people learn in school is not qualitatively different from the way they learn in other parts of life. As they move through the day, students face problems which cause them to go through the "complete act of reflective thought." The resultant use of their intelligence causes growth, and that growth enables them to interact with, and adapt to, their changing world. Their developing ideas become instruments for successful living.

Teachers in a pragmatic educational context are not teachers in the traditional sense of the word. That is, they are not the ones who "know" what the students will need for the future and therefore have the function of imparting such essential bodies of knowledge to their students. For one thing, claims the pragmatist, no one "knows" what students will need, since we live in a world that is constantly changing. This fact, coupled with the idea that there are no such things as *a priori* or absolute truths which all students must know, modifies the role of the teacher.

Teachers in a pragmatic school can be seen as fellow learners in the educational experience, as their entire classes daily face a changing world. Teachers, however, are more experienced fellow travelers and can therefore be viewed as guides or project directors. They advise and guide student activities that have arisen out of the felt needs of their students; and they perform this role in the context of, and with the benefit of, their wider experiences. But, it is essential to note, they do not base class activities on their own felt needs.

Traditional educational philosophies put subject matter at the center of the educational focus. The child was supposed to conform to the demands of the structure of the several curricular areas. Pragmatism rejected that approach and placed students and their needs and interests on center stage. Subject matter, it claims, should be chosen with an eye to the needs of the student.

The curriculum, according to Dewey and other pragmatists, should not be divided into restrictive and unnatural subject-matter areas. It should rather be built around natural units that grow out of the pressing questions and experiences of the learners. The specific units of study might vary from one fourth-grade class to the next, but the idea was that the traditional subjects of the school (art, history, math, reading, etc.) could be woven into a problem-solving technique that utilized the innate curiosity of the students to learn the traditional materials as they worked on problems and issues that were of current interest to them in their daily experience.

Methodology, for the pragmatist, centers around giving students a great deal of freedom of choice in seeking out the experiential (learning) situations that will be the most meaningful to them. The classroom (which is viewed not just as a "school" setting, but any place where experiences may be had) is seen in terms of a scientific laboratory where ideas are put to the test to see if they are capable of verification. Field trips, note the pragmatists, have distinct advantages over such activities as reading and audio-visual experiences, since the student has a better chance to participate in firsthand interaction with the environment. It is true that field trips and other actual experiences with the environment are time-consuming. On the other hand, they are seen to be more motivating, since they have intrinsic interest; and they are more meaningful, because they involve people in direct experience, rather than indirect. For example, one learns more about a dairy and cows by going to the barn and milking, smelling, and hearing a cow than by a week of reading and viewing the process on the movie screen. Thus, the methodology of the pragmatists is in direct line with their experiential epistemology. One favorite technique of the pragmatists is the project method, which will be described in chapter V in the discussion of progressivism.

This experiential methodology, it should be noted, does not imply that all pragmatists are opposed to books, libraries, museums, and other organized knowledge resources. Dewey, for example, held that all study "at the outset" should "fall within the scope of ordinary life-experience." As students mature and build a significant knowledge base upon experience, however, they should be able to come to the place where they can learn through indirect and logical approaches to organized subject matter. In other words, the child, according to Dewey, should gradually move from learning based upon direct experiences to vicarious learning methods. These vicarious methods should be all the more meaningful, since they are building upon a knowledge base founded upon significant experiences in everyday life.[4]

The social policy of the school, as viewed by pragmatism, is that of liberalism in the sense that pragmatists are not afraid of social change. In fact, they claim that social change is inevitable and that the function of the school should be to teach the younger generation to manage change in a healthy manner. The aim of the school is not to have students memorize a set body of

[4] Dewey, *Experience and Education*, pp. 86-112.

content, but rather to have them learn how to learn, so that they can adapt to the constantly changing world of the present and future. From this perspective, it can be claimed that the curriculum of the pragmatic school will be more concerned with process than content.

The political viewpoint of pragmatism is that of democracy. The pragmatists see the school, ideally, as a democratic living and learning environment in which everyone participates in the decision-making process in anticipation of soon having a wider participation in the decision-making process of the larger society. Societal and school decisions, in this framework, are evaluated in the light of their social consequences, rather than in terms of some hallowed tradition. Social, economic, and political change is viewed as good if it betters the condition of society.

# Existentialism

## Background

Existentialism is one of the newer arrivals on the philosophic scene. It is nearly all a twentieth-century product. In many ways it is more closely related to literature and the arts than it is to formal philosophy. That is undoubtedly due to the fact that it is deeply concerned with the emotions of individuals, rather than being primarily concerned with the intellect.

Existentialism, due to its very nature, is difficult, if not impossible, to define. Walter Kaufmann, one of the more perceptive American existentialists, introduces his *Existentialism from Dostoevsky to Sartre* by noting:

> Existentialism is not a philosophy but a label for several widely different revolts against traditional philosophy. Most of the living "existentialists" have repudiated this label, and a bewildered outsider might well conclude that the only thing they have in common is a marked aversion for each other.[5]

[5] Walter Kaufmann, *Existentialism from Dostoevsky to Sartre*, rev. ed. (New York: New American Library, 1975), p. 11.

Existentialism must not be seen as a "school" of thought in the same sense as the other four philosophic positions that we have studied. Kaufmann has identified the heart of existentialism as: (1) the refusal to belong to any school of thought; (2) the repudiation of the adequacy of philosophic systems and bodies of belief; and (3) a marked dissatisfaction with traditional philosophy as superficial, academic, and remote from life.[6]

Individualism is the central pillar of existentialism. The existentialist does not seek for such things as purpose in the universe. Only man, the individual, has purpose.

Existentialism finds its roots in the works of Søren Kierkegaard (1813-1855) and Friedrich Nietzsche (1844-1900). Both men reacted against the impersonalism and formalism of ecclesiastical Christianity and the speculative philosophy of Hegel. Kierkegaard strove to revitalize Christianity from within by uplifting the place of the individual and the role of personal choice and commitment. Nietzsche, on the other hand, denounced Christianity, declared the death of God, and uplifted his version of the superman.

Existentialism has been particularly influential since World War II. A renewed search for meaning seemed especially crucial in a world that had suffered a prolonged depression and had been torn apart by two global wars of unprecedented magnitude. A further stimulant for the existentialists' renewed search for meaning and significance has been the dehumanizing impact of modern industrialism. Existentialism is largely a revolt against a society that has robbed humanity of its individuality. Influential spokesmen for twentieth-century existentialism include Karl Jaspers, Gabriel Marcel, Martin Heidegger, Jean-Paul Sartre, and Albert Camus.

As a newcomer to the world of philosophy, existentialism has focused mainly on philosophical issues and has not, as yet, made itself too explicit on educational practices. Its relative silence on education has also undoubtedly been influenced by its concern for the individual rather than the social group.

[6] Ibid., p. 12.

74

Exceptions to this neglect of educational topics are found in the works of such writers as Martin Buber, Maxine Greene, George Kneller, and Van Cleve Morris.[7] Existentialists have contended that philosophy is not a speculative activity that can be calmly detached from the matrix of the fundamental realities of death, life, and freedom. Philosophy that relies primarily on the intellect is rejected by existentialist thinkers. Philosophy must be "informed by passion," because it is in states of heightened feeling that ultimate realities are discovered. Thus Miguel de Unamuno can condemn those who do philosophy only with their brains as "definition-mongers" and "professionals of thought."[8]

Existentialism, then, is not a "systematic" philosophy. As a result, existentialism does not communicate to educators a set of rules to be mastered or a program to be institutionalized. On the other hand, it does provide a spirit and attitude that can be applied to the educational enterprise. It is from this perspective that we will look at the underlying philosophy of the existentialist. The reader should realize, when studying the material on existentialism, that existentialists do not generally frame their thought in metaphysical, epistemological, and axiological terms. There is, however, a position from which they speak. It is in this cautious spirit that the following analysis is made—with the realization that existentialist thinkers would object to any analysis. This task is performed for philosophic neophytes who need the starting point that can be provided by analysis and labeling if they are to gain a basis from which to develop insight and make evaluations and comparisons.

[7] Martin Buber, *Between Man and Man* (London: Kegan Paul, 1947); Maxine Greene, *Teacher as Stranger: Educational Philosophy for the Modern Age* (Belmont, Calif.: Wadsworth Publishing Co., 1973); George Kneller, *Existentialism and Education* (New York: John Wiley & Sons, 1958); Van Cleve Morris, *Existentialism in Education: What It Means* (New York: Harper & Row, 1966).

[8] Miguel de Unamuno, *Tragic Sense of Life*, trans., J. E. C. Flitch (New York: Dover Publications, 1954), p. 14.

## Philosophic Position of Existentialism

*Reality as existence.* Individual existence is the focal point of existentialism's view of reality. One way to look at the metaphysical foundation of existentialism is to contrast it with the neo-scholastic dictum that essence precedes existence in relation to time. For example, some neo-scholastics have looked upon God as the Creator of all things—including man. When God made man, they claim, He had the idea of man (his essence) in mind before actually creating him.[9]

Existentialism begins by reversing this priority, so that existence precedes essence. Man first is, and then he must attempt to define his whatness or essence. He is faced with such questions as "Who am I?" and "What is the meaning of existence?" in a world that gives no answers. The act of daily living is a process of defining his essence. As he goes through life, he makes choices and develops preferences and dislikes. It is through this activity that he defines who he is as an individual. Through this process he comes to the realization that he is what he chooses to be. He faces an existence that he had no voice in accepting, and he is confronted by the absolute and inescapable necessity of making responsible choices.

The focus of reality resides within the self of the individual human person. Existing is the focal point of the existentialist's philosophy. Man is faced with the stark realities of life, death, and meaning; and he has the unutterable freedom of being responsible for his own essence. He has no external authority upon which to fall back, and he sees philosophic systems as unauthentic cop-outs. The traditional philosophers surrender man's authenticity to a logical system, the Christian leans on God, the realist looks to nature for meaning, and the pragmatist relies on the community. All of these avenues are ways of removing man

[9] In our previous discussions I have sought to avoid what some might interpret as "sexist" statements by using plural nouns and pronouns when referring to teachers and students. That approach, however, is not appropriate in discussing the highly individualistic beliefs of existentialism—a thought world that seemingly demands the singular. As a result, in the discussion of existentialism I have chosen to use such terms as "man," "he," and "him" in a generic sense.

from the frightful reality of being responsible for his choices. They remove the individual from coming to grips with the crucial and primary reality of his own existence and its meaning in a world without meaning apart from that existence. Jean-Paul Sartre, an atheistic existentialist, put man's predicament this way:

> If man, as the existentialist conceives him, is indefinable, it is because at first he is nothing. Only afterward will he be something, and he himself will have made what he will be. Thus, there is no human nature, since there is no God to conceive it. Not only is man what he conceives himself to be, but he is also only what he wills himself to be after this thrust toward existence. Man is nothing else but what he makes of himself. Such is the first principle of existentialism. [10]

Some readers will react to the existentialist perspective with the thought that it doesn't make sense. Many existentialists would not be threatened by that problem; to them life doesn't have to make intellectual sense—in fact, it might even be called "absurd."

*Truth as choice.* Man is the center of epistemological authority in existentialism—not mankind as a species, but man as an individual. Meaning and truth are not built into the universe. Rather, it is man who gives meaning to such things as nature. Note, for example, states the existentialist, how the "laws" of nature have changed through the ages as man has endowed nature with different meanings. Man has a desire to believe in external meanings; and, as a result, he chooses to believe in what he wants to believe.

If existence precedes essence, then first came man, and then came the ideas that man has created. All knowing resides in the individual self, and it is the self that makes the ultimate decision as to what is true. Truth, therefore, can be seen in terms of existential choice, which is based upon the authority of the individual. Even religious existentialists rely on their perception of

[10] Jean-Paul Sartre, *Existentialism and Human Emotions* (New York: Philosophical Library, 1957), p. 15.

personal encounters with the divine rather than on authoritative revelation. This epistemological stance is a radical departure from traditional approaches to religious truth.

*Values from the individual.* The focus of existentialist philosophy is in the realm of axiology, just as the center of traditional philosophy was in metaphysics, and the emphasis of pragmatism was on epistemology. If existential metaphysics can be summed up in the word "existence" and if its concept of epistemology is seen in terms of the word "choice," then it follows that the major portion of life's activities and philosophy's concerns must be bound up in the axiological interests of the individual, who is an existential chooser.

Existentialists are faced with the frightful task of producing values out of nothing. Man has been thrown into life without his consent, and he is free to become whatever he desires. He is not determined. Rather, he is "condemned to be free." Because he is free, he is responsible for his choices and actions. In this vein, Carl Rogers has noted that man cannot rely on either the Bible or the prophets, on Freud or research, nor on the revelations of God or the decisions of other men.[11] Man, the individual, has personal experiences and makes private decisions which are authoritative. Man has no excuse for his actions. Man has, in the idea of Sartre, "no exit" from his freedom and responsibility.

In the realm of ethics there are no absolutes, and there is nobody to spell out the nature of good conduct. If there were such an external authority, life would be much simpler—all man would have to do is comply with the requirements. The anguish of being free to make individual ethical decisions comes about because man must make his own choices and bear responsibility for those choices. He cannot fall back on any source of authority outside of himself.

The anguish of responsible freedom is felt all the more when it is realized that individuals can make choices that are harmful when put into practice. However, if individuals can make harmful choices, they can also make the ethical choices that can

---

[11] Carl R. Rogers, *On Becoming a Person: A Therapist's View of Psychotherapy* (Boston: Houghton Mifflin Co., 1961), p. 24.

counteract those ideas and actions which have proven to be injurious. Man has the great potential of bettering, worsening, or even destroying human existence.

Living the responsible life also includes acting upon one's decisions if a person is to be true or authentic to himself. Unfavorable consequences to a person who acts out his ethical convictions are not the main concern in the eyes of the existentialist. It is important to act regardless of the consequences. The only typically moral question, claims Sartre, is "What, here and now, would be the least *phoney* thing for me to choose?"[12] Not to act is to be irresponsible—it is to seek a world without tension and anguish. Existentialists note that there is no tension after death, but that some people try to make their own lives like death by avoiding conflict at all cost. The opposite of death is life, and life for the existentialist necessitates a degree of tension as a person acts out his ethical convictions.

The aesthetic viewpoint of the existentialist can be described as a revolt from the public standard. Each individual is the supreme court in regard to what is beautiful. As in other areas of existence, no one can make decisions for other individuals. What is beautiful to me is beautiful, and who can contradict me?

## Existentialism and Education

The relative silence of existentialism on education, previously noted, should not be seen as satisfaction with the schools. On the contrary, existentialists are quite disturbed at what they find in the educational establishment. They are quick to note that much of what is called education is nothing but propaganda served to a captive audience. They also point out that much of what currently passes for education is actually harmful, since it prepares a student for consumerism or makes him a cog in the machinery of industrial technology and modern bureaucracy. Instead of helping to bring out individuality and creativity, the

---

[12] Quoted in Mary Warnock, *Ethics Since 1900*, 3d ed. (New York: Oxford University Press, 1978), p. 131.

existentialists cry, much education stifles and destroys these essential human attributes.

In a philosophy that revolts at the regimentation of individuals, it is only to be expected that the individual will be the center of the educational endeavor. Van Cleve Morris claims that existentialist educational concern would focus on helping the individual self come into a fuller realization of the following propositions:

1. I am a *choosing* agent, unable to avoid choosing my way through life.

2. I am a *free* agent, absolutely free to set the goals of my own life.

3. I am a *responsible* agent, personally accountable for my free choices as they are revealed in how I live my life.[13]

The role of the existentialist teacher will not be that of the traditional teacher. The existentialist teacher will not be one who is mainly concerned with cognitive transference and who has the "right" answers. He will rather be a person who is willing to help students explore possible answers.

The teacher will be concerned with the unique individuality of each student. He will realize that no two students are alike, and that, consequently, no two need exactly the same education. The existentialist will seek to relate to every student in what Buber refers to as an "I-Thou," rather than an "I-It," relationship. That is, he will treat the student as an individual with whom he can personally identify, rather than an "It" that needs to be externally directed and filled with knowledge.

The existentialist teacher might be described as what Rogers calls a "facilitator." In this role the teacher will respect the emotional and irrational aspects of individuals and will endeavor to lead his students into a better understanding of themselves. He and the youngsters who are with him will face the ultimate questions of life, death, and meaning as they explore human experiences from a variety of viewpoints. In all of these experiences, both teachers and students will learn and share roles as they

[13] Van Cleve Morris, *Existentialism in Education*, p. 135.

increase in awareness of how to find and be themselves in a mechanized world seeking to rob them of selfhood and individuality.

The curriculum in an existentialist school would of necessity be open to change, since existentialism's concept of truth is ever expanding and changing. From that perspective, student choice should be a deciding factor in the selection of subject matter. That conclusion does not mean, however, that traditional subject matter finds no place in the existentialist's curricular approach. It rather indicates curricular flexibility as opposed to the traditional hierarchy of subjects in terms of importance.

Existentialists are in general agreement that the fundamentals of traditional education—such as the three R's, science, and social studies—should be studied. These so-called basics are the foundation of creative effort and of man's ability to understand himself. These basic subjects, however, should be presented in relation to the student's affective development rather than being isolated from individual meaning and purpose as they often are in traditional education.

The humanities also loom large in the existentialist curriculum, because they give a great deal of insight into the major dilemmas of human existence. The humanities develop themes around people making choices in relation to sex, love, hate, death, disease, and other meaningful aspects of life. They present a total view of man from both a positive and a negative perspective and are therefore superior to the sciences in helping man understand himself.

Beyond the fundamentals and the humanities, the existentialist curriculum is wide open. Any subject that has meaning for an individual can be justified in the course of studies.

Methodology for the existentialists has an infinite number of possibilities. They decry uniformity of materials, curriculum, and teaching, and declare that there should be many options open to students who desire to learn. These options would not have to be restricted to the traditional school, but might be found in alternative types of schools, or in the realm of business, government, or personal affairs. Ivan Illich has put forth some suggestions for educational variations in his *Deschooling Society* (1970) that can be appreciated by many existentialists.

The criteria of existentialist methodology center around the concepts of noncoerciveness and those methods that would help the student to find and be himself. Perhaps the prototypes of existentialist methodology can be viewed through such approaches as Carl Rogers' *Freedom to Learn* (1969) and A. S. Neill's *Summerhill: A Radical Approach to Child Rearing* (1960).

Existentialists are not generally concerned with the social policy of education or the school. Their philosophy lends itself to an emphasis on the individual, rather than to the social aspects of human existence.

## Perspective

The modern philosophies of pragmatism and existentialism, despite their differences, have several points in common. In contrast to the traditional philosophies, both reject *a priori* epistemological considerations and downplay metaphysical ultimates and essences beyond the reach of mankind. In addition, both are relativist in terms of values and truth, and both are humanistic or man-centered. A major difference between pragmatism and existentialism is that the former bases its relativism and humanism on the authority of society, while the latter stresses the role of the individual.

In education, the modern philosophies, in addition to the differences discussed in this chapter, also have likenesses. For example, both see the teacher as being more of a guide or facilitator than an authority figure; both believe the curriculum should center in one way or another around the needs of the child, rather than around a solid core of unchanging "Truth"; and both reject the role of the school as primarily an institution for the transmission of past knowledge to future generations.

Both existentialism and pragmatism have affected twentieth-century education. By far, the largest impact has been made by pragmatism. In fact, the pragmatic influence has made an impression on every aspect of modern education from architecture, movable classroom furniture, and activity centers, to a curriculum at all levels of education that has been broadened to include the practical and useful in addition to the academic. Many observers have noted that pragmatism has "transformed" schooling in the United States and other countries. The impact of existentialism has been more recent and, thus far, less dramatic. Certainly, however, the movements in alternative education, educational humanism, and deschooling that arose in the 1970s found a major portion of their roots in existentialism.

Chapters III and IV have surveyed five traditional and modern philosophies and their relationship to education. In conclusion, a caution that should be emphasized in the study of philosophic systems is that it is not always possible or even desirable to fit either ourselves or formal philosophers into neat little boxes called idealism, realism, or existentialism. These systems, as has been noted, are merely labels to help guide our thinking as we relate to possible answers to the basic issues that have faced mankind through the ages. Chapter V will develop some of the educational extensions of the traditional and modern philosophies as they have been expressed in the twentieth century.

# CONTEMPORARY THEORIES
# OF EDUCATION

# 5

The preceding two chapters discussed five major philosophical viewpoints and the implications of those philosophies for education. The treatment thus far has been an extrapolation of what philosophers have said about education. The present chapter will examine what educators have had to say about their field in the light of philosophy. In other words, this chapter will focus on theories which take educational problems as their starting point and seek answers by appealing to philosophy.

The educational theorists referred to in this chapter have generally not framed their theories in terms of philosophic concerns (i.e., metaphysics, epistemology, and axiology). This does not mean that their educational proposals have no philosophic undergirding. On the contrary, their proposals are thoroughly permeated with assumptions, even though those assumptions may not always be explicit. This chapter, in the spirit of the theorists, will focus on educational principles rather than philosophic categories. Figure 4 illustrates the relationship between the contemporary educational theories and their philosophic roots.

The formulation of these theories has been largely a phenomenon of the twentieth century. Many of their attributes previously existed in an informal manner, but their detailed elaboration has awaited the educational conflict that has been consciously fought in this century.

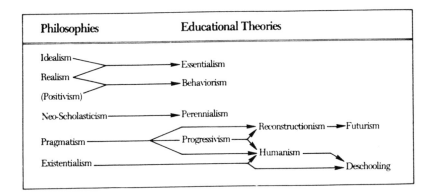

| Philosophies | Educational Theories |
|---|---|

Figure 4
The Relationship of Educational Theories to
Their Philosophic Sources

# Progressivism

## Background

Progressivism in education was part of a larger socio-political movement of general reform that characterized American life in the late-nineteenth and early-twentieth centuries as America sought to adjust to massive urbanization and industrialization. Progressivism in politics was evident in the careers of such leaders as Robert La Follette and Woodrow Wilson, who attempted to curb the power of trusts and monopolies and to make the system of political democracy truly operative. In the social arena, progressives of the stamp of Jane Addams worked in the settlement-house movement to improve social welfare in Chicago and other urban areas. The reforms and attempted reforms of the progressives were many, and educational progressivism must be seen in its wider context.

Progressivism as an educational theory[1] arose as a definite reaction against traditional education, which had emphasized formal methods of instruction, mental learning, and the literary

---

[1] The best history of progressivism in education is found in Lawrence A. Cremin, *The Transformation of the School: Progressivism in American Education, 1876-1957* (New York: Vintage Books, 1964).

classics of Western civilization. The major intellectual influences underlying progressive education were John Dewey, Sigmund Freud, and Jean-Jacques Rousseau. Dewey made his contribution as a philosopher of the pragmatic school who wrote a great deal on the philosophic undergirding of education and attempted to validate his ideas in his laboratory school at the University of Chicago. Pragmatism, therefore, may be seen as a central influence in progressive educational theory. A second influence was the psychoanalytic theory of Freud. Freudian theory bolstered many progressives to argue for more freedom of self-expression among children and a more open learning environment in which children could release the energy of their instinctive impulses in creative ways. A third influence was Rousseau's *Emile* (1762). This book particularly impressed those progressives who were opposed to the interference of adults in establishing the learning goals or curriculum of children. It should be noted that the excesses of the child-centered progressives were more in harmony with the thought of Rousseau and Freud than with that of Dewey, even though Dewey has generally received the blame by the many critics of progressive education.

These underlying intellectual influences were developed into progressive educational theory by a remarkable group of educators who were also active in applying their theory to school practice. Carleton Washburne, William H. Kilpatrick, Harold Rugg, George S. Counts, Boyd H. Bode, and John L. Childs were instrumental in developing the different strains of progressive thought. Through their influence and energy, progressive education became the dominant theory in American education from the 1920s to the 1950s. By the middle of the fifties, when progressive education lost its organizational existence, it had changed the face of American education. Perhaps part of the reason for its organizational demise was the fact that many of its ideas and programs had been adopted, to some extent, by the public school establishment, and the progressives, therefore, had less to "holler" about. From that point of view, it appears that their success led to their dissolution. On the other hand, it should be recognized that progressive theory in its completeness never did become the consistent practice in the vast majority of school systems. What was adopted were bits and pieces of progressivism that were amalgamated with other educational methods in eclectic fashion.

The progressives should not be seen as a group who were unified on all theoretical matters. They were, however, united in their opposition to certain school practices. Allan Ornstein has noted that they generally condemned the following: (1) the authoritarian teacher, (2) heavy reliance on textbooks or bookish methods of instruction, (3) passive learning by memorization of information and factual data, (4) the four-walls approach to education that sought to isolate education from social reality, and (5) the use of fear or physical punishment as a form of discipline.[2]

The major organizational force of progressivism in education was the Progressive Education Association (1919-1955). Progressive education must be seen as both an organized movement and as a theory if one is to understand its history and impact. In both of these aspects it advocated a central core of principles. Many progressive ideas found renewed vitality in the educational humanism of the late 1960s and early 1970s.

## Progressive Principles

*The process of education finds its genesis and purpose in the child.* This position is in direct opposition to the traditional approach to education. The traditional school started with a body of organized subject matter and then sought to impose that corpus of learning on students, whether they desired it or not. The progressives reversed this model by putting the child at the focal point of the school. They then sought to develop a curriculum and teaching method that grew out of students' needs, interests, and initiatives.

According to progressive theory, children have a natural desire to learn and discover things about the world around them. Not only do they have this inborn desire, but they also have certain needs that must be fulfilled in their lives. These desires and needs give children a definite interest in learning those

---

[2] Allan C. Ornstein, *An Introduction to the Foundations of Education* (Chicago: Rand McNally College Publishing Co., 1977), p. 204.

things that will help them solve their problems and thereby fulfill their desires.

Children's interest are, therefore, the natural starting point for the learning experience. That does not mean that children's interests should be the only factor in determining what they should learn. After all, children are still immature and may not be able to define significant purposes. On the other hand, the doctrine of child interest does stipulate that children naturally tend to oppose whatever they feel is imposed on them by others. Child interest, therefore, should be harnessed by the teacher, who will develop a learning environment in which this motivational force will naturally lead to the desired learning outcomes. The teacher uses the children's natural interests to help them learn those skills that will assist them in meeting their current needs and desires. This will, in turn, help students develop problem-solving skills and build the cognitive store of information needed for socialized living.

From the progressive viewpoint, starting with the child is the way that education most easily and naturally takes place. It utilizes the motivational force of genuine child interest and therefore helps students and teachers work together, rather than pitting them against one another in an adversarial relationship. This opens the way for more humaneness in the classroom and allows the teacher to relate to children in all their complexity—as individuals who have needs, desires, feelings, and attitudes.

*Pupils are active rather than passive.* Children are not passive beings who are just waiting for a teacher to stuff their minds full of information. Students are dynamic beings who naturally want to learn and will learn if they are not frustrated in their learning by adults and authorities who seek to impose their wills and goals upon them. Dewey noted that "the child is already intensely active, and the question of education is the question of taking hold of his activities, of giving them direction."[3]

*The teacher's role is that of advisor, guide, and fellow traveler rather than that of authoritarian and classroom director.*

[3] John Dewey, *The School and Society*, rev. ed. (Chicago: University of Chicago Press, 1915), p. 37.

This position is tied closely to both the pragmatists' belief in continual change and the progressives' position on the centrality of the child in education. The teacher cannot be an authority in the traditional sense of being a dispenser of essential information. That is true because a major reality of human existence is change. As a result, no one knows the shape of the future and the essential information that will be needed in the future. Therefore, there can be no authoritative teaching of a restricted body of essential knowledge.

On the other hand, teachers possess greater knowledge and have had more exprience than their students. That puts them in the position of being guides in territory through which they have already passed, advisors in situations in which students reach an impasse, and fellow travelers in those circumstances which are new to them in an ever-changing and ever-evolving world. They are individuals who will learn with their students as they seek to harness student energies and direct student interests in the learning enterprise. The role of teachers can be seen as that of helping students learn how to learn by themselves, so that they will develop into self-sufficient adults in a changing environment.

*The school is a microcosm of the larger society.* The school should not be seen as a distinct social setting in which education takes place in a unique way. Education and learning are constantly taking place in a person's life. For example, a boy watches his father change a tire. He learns from this experience because of his felt need, his natural curiosity, and his interest. This is a learning experience, and learning experiences take place in the same manner inside of schools as they do in the world at large. Learning and educative experiences in the everyday world are not artificially divided into cubicles of time, space, and content. Therefore, the education offered in the schools should not be artificially divided and punctuated by separating English from social studies, or by calling an unnatural halt to an educative experience by ringing the bell at a prearranged time. In the larger world the subject matter of social studies, English, and math is integrated in its usage, and individuals stay at a task until they complete it or come to a natural break.

Education in schools should be seen in terms of how people are educated and learn in the larger world around them, because meaningful education is life itself and does not take on a distinct nature inside the walls of a school. That position is a departure from that of the traditionalists, who see education as a period of preparation for life—a time when the minds of children are being filled with the information they will need for real living.

***Classroom activity should focus on problem solving rather than on artificial methods of teaching subject matter.*** This position rests upon the pragmatists' emphasis on experience and their problem-solving epistemology. Knowledge, declare the progressives, does not come through the reception of information as an abstract substance that is somehow transferred from the teacher to the pupil. Knowledge, they claim, is an instrument for managing experience.

That conclusion is not a rejection of traditional subject matter, but it is a rejection of the traditional method of attempting to transfer that subject matter to the younger generation. The progressives based their curricular and teaching approaches on problems of significance to their students. In doing this they developed the project method of instruction.

The project method can be illustrated by a fourth-grade class that wants to study Indians and decides to build an Indian village. In the process of building their village they run across many problems. For example, they have to decide what kind of Indians they want to be. That problem leads them into the realm of reading, and then into geography and anthropology, as they discover that different tribes related to their environment in varying ways. If they decide to build a tepee, they will have an industrial experience in tanning leather, a geometrical experience in developing the pattern, a mathematical experience as they make the measurements, a biological experience in deciding what type of wood will be best for the poles, and a writing experience when they compose a report concerning their accomplishments.

From this short (and incomplete) example, it is evident that building the village would present the children with a series of problems which they would be interested in solving, since the decision to study Indians had been theirs in the first place. The process of solving these problems would allow a skillful teacher-guide to lead the students through a large part of the traditional curriculum in an almost painless manner. Through the problem-solving process, the students would not only have learned facts; but, more importantly, they would have learned how to think and how to use their thoughts in the world of experience. A project might be as short as three days or as long as a year, depending on the nature of the project, the perseverance of the students, and the skill of the teacher.

*The social atmosphere of the school should be cooperative and democratic.* This position is a natural outgrowth of the progressive belief that the school is a microcosm of the larger society and that education is life itself rather than a preparation for living. The schools, claim the progressives, are unnaturally competitive. In the world of work, if a person has a problem, he or she is generally allowed to seek help from a fellow worker. In the school, however, children are punished for moving about, talking, or even trying to help one another solve a problem. The emphasis in traditional education places an undue emphasis on competition that is neither socially healthy nor educationally efficient. Competition has its place if it serves the general good, but society and learning are more often advanced through cooperation.

Democratic forms of school and classroom direction and control were also advocated by the progressives. They were ardent supporters of political democracy, and they noted that students could not be prepared for democratic adulthood if they were raised in autocratic educational institutions. The school should promote student government, the free discussion of ideas, and the involvement of students and faculty in both learning and educational planning.

# Educational Humanism in Relation to Progressivism

## Background

Organized progressivism came to an end in the mid-fifties, but the ideas of the progressives have continued to make

91

themselves felt through a diversified movement generally referred to as educational humanism. The humanists have adopted most of the progressive principles, including child-centeredness, the non-authoritative role of the teacher, the focus on the active and involved pupil, and the cooperative and democratic aspects of education.

Progressivism, however, is not the only source of educational humanism. Existentialism has also acted as a stimulus for the movement. As a result, educational humanism has placed even more stress on the uniqueness of the individual child than did the progressives, who tended to think of children more in terms of social units. The existentialist strain in educational humanism has led to an emphasis on a search for personal meaning in human existence.

This focus on the individual child in humanistic education has been strengthened even more by a third major contributor to educational humanism—the humanistic or existential psychologists. Psychologists of this strain include such people as Carl Rogers, Abraham Maslow, and Arthur Combs. These psychologists, along with many of their colleagues, have made a direct and significant impact upon humanistic education. Their focus has been on helping the student become "humanized" or "self-actualized"—helping the individual student discover, become, and develop his or her real self and full potential.

A fourth stimulus for educational humanism has been the romantic critics. These writers arose in the social turbulence of the 1960s in a storm of protest over the repressive, mindless, and inhumane conditions of modern schools. They argued that schools had become intellectually deadening and psychologically destructive because they were preoccupied with order and punishment rather than human health and growth. Typical of their genre of educational writing are John Holt's *How Children Fail* (1964), Herbert Kohl's *36 Children* (1967), Jonathan Kozol's *Death at an Early Age* (1967), and George Dennison's *The Lives of Children* (1969). The literature produced by the romantic critics was eloquent, poignant, and popular. As such, it made a large impact on the reading public and developed a grassroots sympathy for experimentation in humanistic education.

## Humanistic Principles

The present discussion of educational humanism will not seek to give a detailed summary of humanistic principles, since that would of necessity include much of the material surveyed in the treatment of progressivism. It will rather highlight humanistic emphases and examine some of the institutional formats through which the humanists have sought to give expression to their convictions.

Central to the humanistic movement in education has been a desire to create learning environments in which children would be free from intense competition, harsh discipline, and the fear of failure. The humanists sought to move away from the adversary relationship so often found between students and teachers, and, on the other hand, to create educational relationships permeated with trust and a sense of security. It was their belief that such an atmosphere would free students from destructive and energy-consuming fears and would allow more energy to be expended toward individual growth and the development of creativity. Holt captured the humanistic view of human nature as it relates to learning when he wrote

> that children are by nature smart, energetic, curious, eager to learn, and good at learning; that they do not need to be bribed and bullied to learn; that they learn best when they are happy, active, involved, and interested in what they are doing; that they learn least, or not at all, when they are bored, threatened, humiliated, frightened.[4]

In short, the humanists sought to move beyond the "jail mentality" of most schools in an attempt to provide learning environments that would lead to individual growth. Hence, the fundamental purpose of education for the humanists centered on self-actualization rather than a mastery of knowledge as an end in itself. As a result, openness, the use of imagination, and experimentation in fantasy were encouraged, while standardized

[4] John Holt, *Freedom and Beyond* (New York: Dell Publishing Co., Laurel Edition, 1972), p. 10.

93

testing and mass teaching were frowned upon. The humanists proposed that teachers could most easily reach their ends through working with individuals and small groups. True to its existential root, educational humanism was seeking to avoid the herd orientation of modern society.

## Institutional Formats

The emphasis on individuality by the humanistic educators has spawned a great deal of diversity in approaches to schooling. Three of the most influential approaches have been the open classroom, the free school, and schools without failure. These became widespread alternatives to traditional educational approaches in the late 1960s and early 1970s.

The open classroom provides a schooling experience that seeks to break up the rigidity of the traditional classroom. The open classroom is a decentralized classroom in which the desks are separated into clusters and space is divided into learning areas. These areas are separated by screens, bookcases, and other objects. Such a classroom might have activity areas for reading, math, and art. Each area would be equipped with a variety of learning materials which the students could use, manipulate, or read as needed. The open classroom does not have a rigid schedule in terms of either time or materials to be covered. Ample provision is made for student cooperation and physical mobility. The teacher and teacher aides generally spend their time with individuals and small groups rather than with the entire class. The open classroom seeks to provide a learning community in which both teachers and students work together. Kohl notes that in the open classroom

> the role of the teacher is not to control his pupils but rather to enable them to make choices and pursue what interests them. In an open classroom a pupil functions according to his sense of himself rather than what he is expected to be. It is not that the teacher should expect the same of all his pupils. On the contrary, the teacher must learn to perceive differences, but these should

emerge from what actually happens in the classroom during the school year, and not from preconceptions.[5]

The free school movement can be seen largely as a revolt from a public education that cannot provide the proper conditions for humanistic education because of its custodial (baby-sitting) and indoctrination functions.[6] The free schools have been developed by dissatisfied parents and teachers who want to get their children away from an authoritative system with its emphasis on a structured curriculum and demands of conformity. Free schools have been established in all types of locations, from slum storefronts to converted army barracks and barns. No two of these schools are alike, and each has its own reason for existence. Most of them are quite small, and their mortality rate has been extremely high—many have lasted for only one or two years. Free schools have appealed to varied social groups, from suburban whites to inner-city blacks. "Some seem to be pastoral escapes from the grit of modern conflict, while others are deliberate experiments in integrated multicultural, multilingual education." All of them seek to develop "free children," who will be independendent and courageous people who will be able to deal with the changing complexities of the modern world.[7]

William Glasser, the psychiatrist who developed "reality therapy," has proposed a humanistic approach to education in his *Schools Without Failure*. Glasser holds that there are two kinds of human failure—"failure to love and failure to achieve self-worth."[8] Schools have traditionally failed, according to Glasser, because they have not established warm interpersonal relationships through which the students' need for love and a sense of self-worth has been satisfied. The role of the school should be to

---

[5] Herbert R. Kohl, *The Open Classroom: A Practical Guide to a New Way of Teaching* (New York: New York Review, 1969), p. 20.

[6] Jonathan Kozol, *Free Schools*, (Boston: Houghton Mifflin Co., 1972), p. 14.

[7] Bonnie Barrett Stretch, "The Rise of the 'Free School,'" in *Curriculum: Quest for Relevance*, 2d ed., ed. William Van Til (Boston: Houghton Mifflin Co., 1974), p. 113.

[8] William Glasser, *Schools Without Failure* (New York: Harper & Row, Perennial Library, 1975), p. 14.

provide a warm and nonthreatening environment in which those needs can be met. This atmosphere will provide an effective context for learning. *Schools Without Failure* provides some detailed suggestions as to how such goals might be reached.

The open classroom, the free school, and schools without failure are just three of the many variations proposed by the educational humanists to humanize schooling. It should be noted that most of the humanistic proposals have been aimed at elementary education.

# Perennialism

## Background

Perennialist educational theory arose as a formal position in the 1930s as a reaction against the progressives, who the perennialists felt were destroying the intellectual fabric of American life by their emphasis in the schools on child-centeredness, presentism, and life adjustment. Modern perennialism generally represents a wholesale rejection of the progressive perspective.[9] For the perennialist, permanence, despite significant social and political upheavals, is more real than the pragmatists' concept of change. The perennialists, therefore, spearheaded a return to the absolutes and focused on the time-honored ideas of human culture—those ideas that had proven their validity and usefulness by having withstood the test of time. Perennialism stressed the importance of mind, reason, and the great works of the intellectual past. Perennialism was traditional, classical education in a revived form that was more specific in its theoretical formulations because it now had a visible and powerful enemy in educational progressivism.

[9] A prominent exception to this generalization is Jacques Maritain, a Roman Catholic philosopher, who, in *Education at the Crossroads* (pp. 12-14), commends progressive education for its methodological advances, but faults it on its lack of educational ends. As noted below, Mortimer J. Adler's *Paideia Proposal* (1983) seems to have taken a softer look at Dewey's contribution than did traditional perennialism, but one gets the impression that Adler merely selected those progressive insights that could be utilized to further his own program.

The key to understanding the perennialist protest is the concept of liberal education. Liberal education in the classical tradition revolved around those studies that made people free and truly human, as opposed to the training that people received to do specific tasks in the world of work. In the Greek world, people were divided into two groups—those who worked and those who thought. It was believed that those who worked performed an essentially animal function, since they relied upon their muscles. On the other hand, those who thought used the distinctively human capacity of rationality. Individuals in the latter group were free individuals who were fit to govern. Since they were free, they needed an education that would develop their human—rational—capacity. Education, therefore, focused on the rational and mental aspect of humanity and tended to dwell on the influential ideas of Western culture. Training for work was not seen as an educational task; and, as a result, it was nearly always obtained through apprenticeship rather than schooling. Formal education through schooling was left to bestow its attention on developing the free or liberal person. Thus the liberal arts formed the curriculum in traditional education.

The liberal arts educational tradition was passed from Greece to Rome and from Rome to Christian Europe. Up until the late-nineteenth and early-twentieth centuries it represented the main line of education in Europe and the United States. The rise of industrialism, however, brought problems and changes to education. The machine freed more people from the task of the "slave" and provided a base of wealth that enabled them to partake of the educational privileges that had once been restricted to the ruling classes. Traditional education, however, did not enlist the interest of, and did not seem to be of meaning for, many of the people who came from working-class backgrounds. The progressives had arisen in an attempt to make education more meaningful to the new masses in the schools. By the 1930s the traditionalists were ready to take a stand on what they considered to be the threat of anti-intellectualism in the American schools. Their basic position was that machines could do for every modern person what slavery did for the fortunate few of Athens. In a democracy, therefore, all people could be free and rulers. Thus all people needed a liberal education so that they could think and communicate, rather than just a training for animal existence through schooling for work.[10]

The two most influential spokesmen for the perennialists have been Robert Maynard Hutchins and Mortimer J. Adler, who led their campaign from the University of Chicago, where Hutchins became president in 1929 at the age of thirty. Both men were active lecturers and writers and sought to mold public opinion in favor of perennialism for over forty years. Hutchins and Adler made a major contribution for the perennialists when they undertook the editing of the massive collection entitled *Great Books of the Western World*. That collection consists of about one hundred of the works of the West that contain the "best" in ideas and thought. The perennialist educational position found its purest implementation at St. John's College in Annapolis, Maryland, where President Stringfellow Barr made the study of the great books the basis for the bachelor's degree. The late 1980s saw a forceful plea for perennialism in higher education in the form of Allan Bloom's best-selling book, *The Closing of the American Mind* (1987).

Philosophically, perennialism finds its roots in neo-scholasticism. It therefore relies heavily on the thought of Aristotle. Perennialism in America has been largely associated with secular education, even though neo-scholasticism rests upon the writings of Thomas Aquinas as well as upon those of Aristotle. Roman Catholic educational theory has many affinities to the secular mainstream of perennialism, but it lays more emphasis on the spiritual, the theological, and Thomistic thought. The educational writings of Jacques Maritain are representative of perennialism's ecclesiastical branch.

Up through the early 1980s, perennialism had made most of its recommendations with the secondary school, and especially the college, in mind. The role of elementary education was seen as that of providing students with tools that they could later use to study and understand the liberal tradition. The year 1982,

---

[10] Robert M. Hutchins, *The Learning Society* (New York: New American Library, 1968), p. 165.

however, saw the publication of *The Paideia Proposal,* in which a group led by Adler set forth an agenda and a program directly aimed at "basic schooling" for the first twelve years of American education. While the Paideia Group gave at least outward lip service to some of the insights of John Dewey, the findings of educational psychology, and the exigencies of modern society, its recommendations were in harmony with traditional perennialist concerns and goals.[11]

## Perennialist Principles

*Man is a rational animal.* As previously noted, those with perennialist presuppositions see people as largely sharing with the animal world many desires, enjoyments, and tasks. For instance, dogs enjoy riding in cars, can carry burdens and do other forms of work, and relish food that has been prepared for humans. In this sense, mankind and the animals share much in common. What makes mankind distinctly human is the fact that, of all the animals, only humans possess a rational intellect. This is humanity's most unique and valuable characteristic. Aristotle claimed that man is a rational animal, and perennialists share that viewpoint. Their view of education, therefore, focuses on the education of the rational part of people. Hutchins noted that "one thing is essential to becoming human, and that is learning to use the mind."[12] As individuals develop their minds, they can then use their reason to control their appetites and passions.

*Human nature is universally consistent; therefore, education should be the same for everyone.* One important fact about the rational nature of mankind is that it has been shared by all persons throughout all periods of human history. If humans are rational animals, and if people are universally the same in this

---

[11] See Mortimer J. Adler, *The Paideia Proposal: An Educational Mainifesto* (New York: Macmillan Publishing Co., 1982); Mortimer J. Adler, *Paideia Problems and Possibilities* (New York: Macmillan Publishing Co., 1983); Mortimer J. Adler, ed., *The Paideia Program: An Educational Syllabus* (New York: Macmillan Publishing Co., 1984).

[12] Hutchins, *The Learning Society,* p. 114.

respect, then it follows that all people should have the same education. On this point, Hutchins wrote:

> Every man has a function as a man. The function of a citizen or a subject may vary from society to society, and the system of training, or adaptation, or instruction, or meeting immediate needs may vary with it. But the function of a man as man is the same in every age and in every society, since it results from his nature as a man. The aim of an educational system is the same in every age and in every society where such a system can exist: it is to improve man as man.[13]

*Knowledge is universally consistent; therefore, there are certain basic subject matters that should be taught to all people.* If knowledge were not the same everywhere, learned people would not be able to agree on anything. Individuals may have different opinions, but when they do agree, opinion becomes knowledge. The educational system should deal with knowledge, not opinion, because knowledge leads people to eternal truth and acquaints the student with the world's permanencies. Hutchins set forth the curricular uniformity of education in the following deduction: "Education implies teaching. Teaching implies knowledge. Knowledge is truth. The truth is everywhere the same. Hence education should be everywhere the same."[14]

Education, claim the perennialists in opposition to the progressives, should not adjust individuals to the world, but rather adjust them to the truth. The curriculum should not focus on students' immediate interests, what seems important at the moment, or what may appeal to a particular society in a unique time and place. Nor is vocational or professional training a function of education. The school should focus on educating the intellect to grasp and understand the essential and eternal truths that relate to the role of individuals in human society. This shared knowledge base will help people understand one another and will

---

[13] Robert M. Hutchins, *The Conflict in Education* (New York: Harper and Brothers, 1953), p. 68.

[14] Hutchins, *The Higher Learning in America*, p. 66.

better equip them to communicate and build a more satisfactory social order.

*The subject matter, not the child, should stand at the center of the eductional endeavor.* Most perennialists are in agreement that if the educational system is to acquaint the student with eternal truth, it will have to have a curriculum emphasizing languages, history, mathematics, natural science, philosophy, and the fine arts.

The focal point of learning in perennialism lies in activities designed to discipline the mind. Difficult mental exercises, including reading, writing, drill, rote memory, and computation, are significant in training and disciplining the intellect. Learning to reason is also important. Thus exercises in grammar, logic, and rhetoric are imperative activities. These tasks may be somewhat distasteful to the average student, but even that is beneficial, since the will is developed as students persevere in hard intellectual tasks. The externally enforced mental discipline of the classroom helps children internalize the will power that will later be needed as they face difficult tasks in adult life, when there is no "enforcer" to urge them to complete unpleasant duties.

*The great works of the past are a repository of knowledge and wisdom which has stood the test of time and is relevant in our day.* The great books program associated with Hutchins, Adler, and St. John's College has been the avenue through which perennialism has received its widest publicity, even though not all leaders in the movement support the program. Those who endorse the great books approach maintain that studying the works of the leading minds down through history is the best means of coming into contact with the greatest ideas of mankind and of thereby developing the intellect.

The greatness of a book lies in its status as a classic. A classic is a work relevant to every age, and is therefore superior to culture's lesser works. Those works which belong to this category are those that have stood the test of time. Since these books have been found valuable in varying centuries, civilizations, and cultures, they must contain a great deal of truth. If that assumption is valid, claim the perennialists, then the study of such

101

works is imperative. Adler noted that the reading of the great books

> is not for antiquarian purposes; the interest is not archaeological or philological. . . . Rather the books are to be read because they are as contemporary today as when they were written, and that because *the problems they deal with and the ideas they present are not subject to the law of perpetual and interminable progress.*[15]

This emphasis on reading the original great works is in opposition to the essentialist tradition in education, which has uplifted the textbook as the major way to transmit organized subject matter. Hutchins stated that "textbooks have probably done as much to degrade the American intelligence as any single force. If the student should know about Cicero, Milton, Galileo, or Adam Smith, why should he not read what they wrote?"[16]

Those perennialists who do not favor the great books program maintain that contemporary sources of great ideas may be used to acquire knowledge. They are, however, just as concerned that students deal directly with the great intellects, rather than with the predigested mental food contained in textbooks.

*The educational experience is a preparation for life, rather than a real-life situation.* By its very nature the school is an artificial arrangement in which immature intellects become acquainted with mankind's greatest achievements. The school is not, and should not be, as the progressives would have it, a microcosm of the larger society. Human life, in its fullest sense, can be lived only after the rational part of a person is developed. The school is a specialized institution that seeks to accomplish this all-important mission. It is not concerned with such things as

[15] Mortimer J. Adler, "The Crisis in Contemporary Education," *Social Frontier* 5 (February 1939): 144.

[16] Hutchins, *The Higher Learning in America*, pp. 78-79. It should be noted that the thrust of the argument for the use of the great books is aimed at higher education rather than at the elementary level. It seems that even those perennialists most enthusiastic about the great books in high school and college would grant the necessity of using textbooks to gain the tools of learning in such areas as mathematics and grammar. See, e.g., Adler, *Paideia Proposal*, pp. 23, 24.

the occupational, amusement, and recreational aspects of humanity. These have their place in the life of people, but they lie outside the proper activities of educational institutions.

# Essentialism

## Background

A second reaction to progressivism in education also arose in the 1930s under the banner of essentialism. Essentialists agreed with the perennialists that progressive educational practice was too "soft," since, in its attempt to make learning a painless enterprise, it had moved away from the difficult problem of grappling with the educational basics, such as the mastery of the tools of learning (the three R's) and the established facts. On the other hand, the approach of the perennialists appeared to be too aristocratic for many Americans and, to some observers, even smacked of anti-democratic ideals.

Essentialists, unlike the progressives and perennialists, do not have a singular philosophic base. The underlying philosophies of essentialism are idealism and realism. In addition, the essentialist tradition also contains a large number of "concerned citizens," who feel that the schools have "gone to pot" and that they need to get back to stricter discipline and a study of the "basics."

Essentialism forms the main stream of popular educational thought in most countries, including the United States. It is a conservative position and, as a result, is more concerned with the school's function of transmitting tested facts and truth than it is with innovation and educational frills.

Since the 1930s the essentialists have put forth a great deal of effort to warn the American public of "life-adjustment education," the child-centered school, and the deterioration of learning in the United States. In 1938 a major voice was organized in the form of the Essentialist Committee for the Advancement of American Education under the leadership of William C. Bagley, Isaac L. Kandel, and Frederick Breed. A second major essentialist organization was formed in the 1950s as the Council for Basic Education. The leading spokesmen for this group were Mortimer Smith and Arthur Bestor.

The general position of the Council can be viewed through the titles of Bestor's important works on education—*Educational Wastelands: The Retreat from Learning in Our Public Schools* (1953) and *The Restoration of Learning: A Program for Redeeming the Unfulfilled Promise of American Education* (1955). Bestor's remark that "the men who drafted our constitution were not trained for the task by 'field trips' to the mayor's office and the county jail" is representative of essentialism's critique of progressivism's "contribution" to American education.[17] The Council for Basic Education was not only concerned with the deterioration of American public education, but it was also skeptical of the value of formal educational studies by professional specialists in education.

Another influential essentialist spokesman was Admiral Hyman G. Rickover, father of the atomic submarine, who deplored the lack of developed minds in America. He recommended the adoption of a European-type educational system, such as that of the Dutch or the Russians, so that American youth would have a good grasp of the basics upon high-school graduation and would be adequately prepared to enter an intensive and rigorous professional or technological course of study.

The launching of *Sputnik* in 1957 added weight to the essentialist campaign, since many Americans interpreted the Soviet success as an indication of American educational inferiority. As a result, the late fifties and early sixties saw massive programs of curricular revision. New approaches to the teaching of mathematics, linguistics, science, and other areas of knowledge became important.

At the other end of the continuum of educational reform, however, the sixties also saw a powerful movement to humanize the schools along progressive lines. The predictable reaction to the new wave of educational humanism was a renewed call back

---

[17] Quoted in Henry J. Perkinson, *The Imperfect Panacea: American Faith in Education, 1865-1976*, 2d ed. (New York: Random House, 1977), p. 93.

to the basics, a call that became progressively strident throughout the 1970s. By the early 1980s the United States government had entered the fray. In 1983 the National Commission on Excellence in Education issued an evaluation of American education entitled *A Nation at Risk: The Imperative for Educational Reform.*

The report warned that "the educational foundations of our society are presently being eroded by a rising tide of mediocrity that threatens our very future as a Nation and a people."[18] The report called for renewed emphasis on the "Five New Basics," which would include, as minimun standards for high-school graduation, four years of English, three years of mathematics, three years of science, three years of social studies, and one-half year of computer science. It also recommended two years of foreign language for college-bound students.[19]

*A Nation at Risk* stimulated several other national reports that emphasized the need to return to the teaching of basic subjects and skills in the schools. Among these were the College Board's *Academic Preparation for College: What Students Need to Know and Be Able to Do* (1983) and a report by the Task Force on Education for Economic Growth entitled *Action for Excellence: A Comprehensive Plan to Improve Our Nation's Schools* (1983).[20]

Besides the drive in the 1970s and early 1980s to get back to the academic basics, the right wing of American Protestantism opened up a drive to get the basic of all basics—religion—back into the school curriculum. Upset with the Supreme Court rulings against Bible reading and prayer in the public schools, and shocked by the moral breakdown of American culture in the 1960s, fundamentalist leaders such as Jerry Falwell and Tim

[18] National Commission on Excellence in Education, *A Nation at Risk*, p. 5.

[19] Ibid., p. 24.

[20] For treatments of the "excitement" stirred up by the latest back-to-the-basics movement, see Beatrice and Ronald Gross, eds., *The Great School Debate: Which Way for American Education?* (New York: Simon & Schuster, 1985); William W. Wayson et al., *Up from Excellence: The Impact of the Excellence Movement on Schools* (Bloomington, Indiana: Phi Delta Kappa Educational Foundation, 1988).

LaHaye crusaded not only to get the three R's back into the classroom, but especially to get the fourth R—religion—into the center of education. As they saw it, educational humanism was a threat that paled into relative insignificance in the face of the peril of its underlying philosophy of "secular humanism." The upshot was not only a drive to put religion back into the public classroom, but the creation of thousands of Christian day schools by conservative Protestant groups that had traditionally supported the public system. By the early 1980s the new wave of Christian day schools was perhaps the most rapidly growing sector of American education.[21]

Essentialism, like other theories, does not find all of its proponents in total agreement as to the best course for the schools, but they are in agreement on several major principles.

## Essentialist Principles

*The school's first task is to teach basic knowledge.* For the essentialists, education finds its center in the teaching and learning of the basic skills and subject matters that will, upon their mastery, prepare the student to function as a member of a civilized society. The elementary school, according to the essentialists, should focus its attention on a curriculum engineered to cultivate the basic tool skills that contribute to literacy and the mastery of arithmetical computations. Thus the three R's—the elementary essentials—are stressed. The secondary curriculum would aim at developing competency in history, mathematics, science, English, literature, and foreign languages. The essentialist program implies that educational nonessentials, such as tap dancing and basket weaving, are not the business of the school. The school should aim at teaching the hard core of fundamental learning to all youth.

[21] Jerry Falwell, *Listen, America!* (Garden City, N.Y.: Doubleday & Co., 1980); Tim LaHaye, *The Battle for the Mind* (Old Tappan, N.J.: Fleming H. Revell, 1980); James C. Carper, "The Christian Day School," in *Religious Schooling in America*, eds. James C. Carper and Thomas C. Hunt (Birmingham, Alabama: Religious Education Press, 1984), pp. 110-29.

Essentialists are outraged by the fact that many high-school graduates are functionally illiterate and that a large number of college freshmen need "bonehead" English. Schools, they claim, have catered too long to the desires of the students. That has made a farce of education. What children need is to get to know the world as it really is by coming to grips with basic and essential subject matter.

*Learning is hard work and requires discipline.* Learning those things that are essential cannot always be related to the interest of the child. Although progressivism's problem-solving approach to learning is often helpful, it should be recognized that not all subject matter can be broken up into problems and projects. Much of it will have to be learned by such straightforward methods as memorization and drill. The immediate needs of the child are not as important as more distant goals. Effort is more important than interest, even though interest should be used as a motivational force whenever it is evident. For many students, interest develops as they put forth the amount of effort necessary to understand a field of subject matter.

Students, like adults, are easily diverted from tasks that take effort. They need, therefore, to discipline themselves to focus their attention on the task at hand. Many students, however, do not have this ability and need the assistance of a teacher who can tactfully provide an external context that will help them get down to the hard work of performing a difficult assignment.

*The teacher is the locus of classroom authority.* The essentialists hold that the teacher is not a fellow learner or a guide. Rather, the teacher is one who knows what the students need to know and is well acquainted with the logical order of the subject matter and the way it should be presented.

In addition, the teacher, as a representative of the adult community, is in a position that demands respect. If this respect is not forthcoming, the teacher has the right and responsibility to administer disciplinary measures that will lead to an atmosphere conducive to orderly learning.

107

## Essentialism and Perennialism Compared

In our discussion of essentialism and perennialism it has been seen that these two conservative theories have a great deal in common. Christopher Lucas has expressed their commonality in the following manner:

> First, traditionalists or conservatives of varied persuasions have tended to agree that considerations of technocratic utility and efficiency should be subordinated to the paramount intellectual, spiritual, and ethical purposes of general education. Secondly, essentialists and perennialists concur that the crux of the educational enterprise is the transmission and assimilation of a prescribed body of subject matter, one incorporating the basic elements of the social cultural heritage. Thirdly, both groups acknowledge the cardinal importance of effort, discipline, and self-control in the learning process, as opposed to self-indulgent gratification of immediate needs and transitory interests. Fourthly, conservatives come together in endorsing the idea of curricular continuity: the foundations for a collegiate-level liberal education are laid in a systematic, planned, and sequential exposure to the rudiments of learning skills, beginning with the three R's in the elementary school and extending through to an orderly introduction to the basic subject matter disciplines at the secondary school level.[22]

Even though there is a large amount of similarity between essentialism and perennialism, there are also several pivotal differences which make them quite distinct as educational theories. These differences have been succinctly summarized by George F. Kneller. One major point of variation, according to Kneller, is that essentialism is less totally intellectual than perennialism. Essentialism is less concerned with the supposedly eternal truths, and is more concerned than perennialism with the adjustment of students to their physical and social environment. A second point of departure is that essentialism is more willing to absorb

[22] Christopher J. Lucas, ed., *Challenge and Choice in Contemporary Education: Six Major Ideological Perspectives* (New York: Macmillan Publishing Co., 1976), p. 14.

the positive contributions of progressivism to educational method. A third area of variance is found in a different attitude to the great works of the past. Perennialists place much more emphasis on these works as timeless expressions of mankind's universal insights. Essentialists, on the other hand, see the great works of the past as one of many possible sources for the study of present problems.[23] A fourth point, one not brought out by Kneller but one that should help the reader to understand better the differences between these two theories, is that the major thrust of perennialism has traditionally been directed at higher education, while the essentialists seem to be primarily concerned with the elementary and secondary levels.

# Reconstructionism

## Background

The 1930s was a decade of crisis. Worldwide depression had crippled the capitalistic nations economically, totalitarianism was raising its head in Europe and Asia, and social unrest was a growing feature in America. To some observers in the United States it appeared that democracy itself might be in its last hour. These observers noted that the depression of the thirties was not a problem of a lack of food or material goods. There was an abundance of those things. The depression has been accurately described as a famine in the midst of plenty. America's problem centered upon the distribution of goods and foodstuffs rather than upon their production. In the early thirties, the business sector was partially paralyzed, and the politicians appeared to be helpless in the face of massive economic disaster.

It was in this context that George S. Counts developed a rousing approach to education through several provocative speeches that in 1932 found their way into print as *Dare the School Build a New Social Order?* Counts called to educators to throw off their slave mentality, to deliberately reach for power, and then to

---

[23] George F. Kneller, *Introduction to the Philosophy of Education*, 2d ed. (New York: John Wiley & Sons, 1971), pp. 60-61.

make the most of their conquest by helping to shape a new social order based on a collective economic system and democratic political principles. He called for the educational profession to organize from the kindergarten through the university and to use their organized power in the interests of the great masses of the people.[24]

This position represented a reversal of the traditional role of the school from being a passive transmitter of the culture to being an active and leading agency of societal reform. The 1930s saw a group known as the "Frontier Thinkers" form around Counts and Harold Rugg at Columbia University. Their ideas were largely an extension of the social aspects of Dewey's progressive thought. The philosophical base of reconstructionism is found in pragmatism.

The postwar period saw a renewed thrust at reconstructionism through the work of Theodore Brameld. Some of Brameld's more influential writings have been *Patterns of Educational Philosophy* (1950), *Toward a Reconstructed Philosophy of Education* (1956), and *Education as Power* (1965).

## Principles of Reconstructionism

*World society is in a state of crisis, and civilization as we know it will come to an end unless current practices are reversed.* The problems of population, pollution, limited natural resources, global inequality in the distribution of resources, nuclear proliferation, racism, nationalism, and the naive and irresponsible uses of technology threaten our present world order and will destroy it if not corrected as soon as possible. These problems, note the reconstructionists, are coupled with the challenge of modern totalitarianism, a loss of humanistic values in a mass society, and the increase of functional ignorance among the world's population. In short, the world is facing economic, military, and social

[24] George S. Counts, *Dare the School Build a New Social Order?* (New York: John Day Co., 1932), pp. 28-30.

110

problems on an unprecedented scale. The problems faced are of such a magnitude that they can no longer be ignored.

*The only effective solution to world problems is the creation of a planetary social order.* Just as the problems are worldwide, so must be the solutions. Total cooperation by all nations is the only hope for a dynamic world population living in a finite world with limited amounts of irreplaceable resources. The technological era has brought about worldwide interdependence as well as great advances in the sciences. On the other hand, we are suffering from cultural lag in adapting to the new world order. We are attempting to live in the age of the space ship with a value system and political mentality forged in the horse-and-buggy era.

According to reconstructionism, mankind now lives in a world society in which technological ability can do away with material wants for all people. In this society, a "utopian" existence is possible as the international community cooperatively moves from a preoccupation with producing and fighting over material goods to a phase in which human needs and interests are considered most important. In such a world, people could concentrate on being better human beings as an end in itself.

*Formal education can become a major agent in the reconstruction of the social order.* Schools that reflect the dominant social values, claim the reconstructionists, will merely transmit the social, economic, and political ills that are currently afflicting mankind. The school can and must reverse its traditional role and become a fountainhead of social innovation. The task of reversing the educational role is urgent, due to the fact that mankind now has the capability of self-annihilation.

The critics of social reconstruction argue that Brameld and his colleagues place too much confidence in the power of teachers and other educators to act as primary instruments of social change. The reconstructionist reply is that the only alternative to social reconstruction is global chaos and the eventual obliteration of human civilization. From their perspective, either education will be an instrument to obscure the urgent necessity of social transformation and thus thwart change, or it will be enlisted as an agent for effecting society's positive and orderly transition into the future.[25]

The reconstructionists do not see the school as having the power to create social change single-handed. On the other hand, they do view the school as a major agent of power that touches the life of the entire society, since it reaches its children during their most impressionable age. As such, it can be a primary instigator of insight into social problems and a foremost agitator for social change.

*Teaching methods must be based upon democratic principles that rely upon the native intelligence of the majority to recognize and act upon the most valid solution to the problems of mankind.* Reconstructionists, like those in other branches of the progressive movement, are unified in their view of democracy as the best political system. From their perspective, it is imperative that democratic procedures be used in the classroom as students are led into opportunities to choose between varying social, political, and economic options.

Brameld uses the term "defensible partiality" to describe the position of teachers in relation to controversial curricular items. In this posture, teachers allow the open examination of evidence that agrees and disagrees with their position, and they present alternative positions as fairly as possible. On the other hand, teachers should not mask their convictions. They should both express and defend their partialities publicly. Beyond that, teachers must work for the acceptance of their viewpoint by the largest possible majority. It seems to be assumed by reconstructionists that the issues are so clear-cut that the majority will agree about both the problems and the solutions if free and democratic dialog is allowed. Some observers have noted that reconstructionism has a great deal of faith in the intelligence and good will of mankind—what some have called a utopian faith.

*If formal education is to be a part of the social solution in the present world crisis, it must actively teach for social change.*

[25] Lucas, *Challenge and Choice in Contemporary Education*, p. 326.

"Teachers," penned Counts, "should deliberately reach for power and then make the most of their conquest."[26] Education must awaken the students' consciousness to social problems and engage them actively in working for a solution. Social consciousness may be awakened if students are encouraged to question the *status quo* and to investigate controversial issues in religion, society, economics, politics, and education. Critical investigation and discussion will help students see the injustice and nonfunctionality of many aspects of the present system. It also will help them develop alternatives to conventional wisdom.

The social sciences of anthropology, economics, sociology, political science, and psychology would form a very helpful curricular foundation from which reconstructionists could identify major problem areas of controversy, conflict, and inconsistency. The role of education would be to expose the problem areas of human culture and to build the widest possible consensus about the primary aims that should govern humanity in the reconstruction of world culture. The ideal world society of reconstructionism would be "under the control of the great majority of the people who are rightly the sovereign determiners of their own destiny."[27]

## Futurism in Relation to Reconstructionism

In 1970 Alvin Toffler, in response to the ever-accelerating explosion of knowledge and technology, raised a new dimension of educational theory in his best-selling *Future Shock*. "What passes for education today, even in our 'best' schools and colleges," claimed Toffler, "is a hopeless anachronism."[28] Schools

---

[26] Counts, *Dare the School Build a New Social Order?*, p. 28.

[27] Theodore Brameld, *Education for the Emerging Age* (New York: Harper & Row, 1961), p. 25.

[28] Alvin Toffler, *Future Shock* (New York: Random House, 1970), p. 353.

are operating on a set of practices and assumptions developed in the industrial era, while society has entered into the age of super-industrialism. As a result, schools are educating youth with an emphasis on the past, while they live in a world order undergoing continuing and accelerating change. Toffler claimed that

> our schools face backward toward a dying system, rather than forward to the emerging new society. Their vast energies are applied to cranking out Industrial Men—people tooled for survival in a system that will be dead before they are.
>
> To help avert future shock, we must create a super-industrial educational system. And to do this, we must search for our objectives and methods in the future, rather than the past.[29]

Toffler stressed the need of the educational system "to generate successive, alternative images of the future," so that students and teachers might have something to direct their attention to in the educational undertaking.[30] Students should examine possible, probable, and preferable futures as they study the future of human society and develop the expertise that will lead, it is hoped, to a preferable future.[31]

The futurists, unlike the reconstructionists, do not claim that schools can directly initiate social change. The aim of the futurists is to help prepare people to respond to change and make choices in an intelligent manner as mankind moves into a future that has more than one possible configuration. In order to do this, however, the futurist, like the reconstructionist, must critically examine the current social, political, and economic order.

Harold Shane has outlined a futurist curriculum that focuses on the injustices, contradictions, and problems in our current world order. The curricular stress and the educational activities

[29]Ibid., p. 354.

[30]Ibid., p. 357.

[31]Cf. George R. Knight, "The Transformation of Change and the Future Role of Education," *Philosophic Research and Analysis*, 8 (Early Spring, 1980), pp. 10-11.

he suggests are similar to what the reconstructionists have put forth, and the results of both systems would be largely the same—to develop "a preferable future" through education.[32] From this perspective, futurism can be seen as an extension and modification of reconstructionism.

An educational movement closely related to both reconstructionism and futurism is the third-world educational program of liberation and development—a revolutionary educational theory that seeks to bring about changes in worldwide culture in favor of a healthier future through grassroots education of the lower classes concerning their political, social, and economic rights and possibilities. At the forefront of this movement was Paulo Freire's *Pedagogy of the Oppressed* (1970)—a truly revolutionary theory of education.

# Behaviorism

## Background

A major force in education since mid-century has been behaviorism. Behaviorism is in one sense a psychological theory, but in another sense it has burst the bounds of traditional psychological concerns and has developed into a full-blown educational theory. As an approach to education, it has been welcomed among those "modern" individuals who treasure scientific methodology and "objectivity," as well as among a sizable sector of the business community that values visible and immediate results, efficiency, and economy.

Behaviorism has several ideological roots. One of these is philosophical realism. With realism, behaviorism focuses on the laws of nature. Mankind, from the behaviorist perspective, is a part of nature and, as a result, operates according to nature's

---

[32] Harold G. Shane, *The Educational Significance of the Future* (Bloomington, Indiana: Phi Delta Kappa, 1973), pp. 83-91. For additional insight into the curricular implications of futurism, see Alvin Toffler, ed., *Learning for Tomorrow: The Role of the Future in Education* (New York: Vintage Books, 1974).

laws. Reality, for the behaviorist, is independent of the human knower. The task of the behaviorist is to observe living organisms, including humans, in an attempt to discover the laws of behavior. After these laws have been discovered, they will provide a foundation for a technology of behavior.

A second root of behaviorism is positivism.[33] The thrust of the positivists was to arrive at what Auguste Comte (1798-1857) described as "positive" knowledge. Comte divided the history of mankind into three epochs, each of which was characterized by a distinct way of thinking. The most primitive epoch is the *theological,* in which things are explained by references to spirits and gods. The middle period is the *metaphysical,* in which events are explained by essences, causes, and inner principles. The highest period is the *positive.* In this last stage people do not attempt to go beyond observable and measurable fact. Comte was seeking to develop a science of society, and the behaviorists have built upon his platform. Their position represents a rejection of essences, feelings, and inner causes that cannot be measured.[34] Empirical verification is central in behavioral methodology.

A third historical root of behaviorism is materialism. Materialism, reduced to its core, is the theory that reality may be explained by the laws of matter and motion. It represents an explicit rejection of beliefs about mind, spirit, and conciousness. These are claimed to be relics of a prescientific age.

Russian psychologist Ivan Pavlov (1849-1936) set the stage for behaviorist psychology through his study of reflex reaction. Pavlov noted that he could condition dogs to salivate by ringing a bell if the dogs had previously been trained to associate the sound of the bell with the arrival of food. The father of modern behaviorism, John B. Watson (1878-1958), following the lead of Pavlov, asserted that human behavior is a matter of conditioned

[33] This philosophical approach will be more fully discussed in chapter VI.

[34] Some writers have accused behaviorism, on the basis of its demand for positive knowledge, of the error of creating mankind into the image of the techniques by which it is studied.

reflexes. Watson postulated that psychology should stop studying what people think and feel, and begin to study what people do. For Watson the environment was the primary shaper of behavior. He held that if a child's environment could be controlled, then he could engineer the child into any type of person desired.

The most influential of the behaviorists has been B. F. Skinner. Skinner's work has been at the forefront of the battle of behaviorism in education in such areas as behavior modification, teaching machines, and programmed learning. Some of Skinner's more influential works have been *Science and Human Behavior* (1953), *Beyond Freedom and Dignity* (1971), and *Walden Two* (1948). Perhaps his utopian novel of a behaviorally engineered society, *Walden Two*, has given his ideas as much publicity as anything he has written. Skinner has been a storm center of controversy, because he repudiates the freedom and dignity traditionally ascribed to human beings and seems to indicate that some individuals should decide how others will be conditioned. This, for his critics, brings frightful visions of George Orwell's *1984* into view. Skinner, however, notes that we are being conditioned by the environment anyway, and that it makes more sense to use the laws of behavioral technology to condition people in such a way as to maximize the chances of human survival in a technologically complex age than to let those laws operate at random.

It should be plain from this short overview of the foundations of behaviorism that it is deeply embedded in the presuppositions of naturalistic science. Behaviorists hope to develop the "science" of humanity. "Behaviorism," however, notes Skinner, "is not the science of human behavior; it is the philosophy of that science."[35] Skinner's statement highlights the fact that there are no sciences without philosophic assumptions—assumptions which shape and limit their potential discoveries. Since this is the case, it is essential that educators be aware of the assumptions of any given theory before they seek to apply those theories in their professional practice.

[35] B. F. Skinner, *About Behaviorism*, (New York: Vintage Books, 1976), p. 3.

## Behaviorist Principles

*Human beings are highly developed animals who learn in the same way that other animals learn.* For behaviorists, mankind does not stand above and outside of nature. Humans are not beings who are in a class by themselves. Mankind is rather a part of nature. According to Skinner, "a small part of the universe is contained within the skin of each of us. There is no reason why it should have any special physical status because it lies within this boundary."[36] Humans do not have any special dignity or freedom. It is true that a person is a complex natural organism, but an individual is still primarily a part of the animal kingdom. Behaviorism is unapologetically evolutionary, and that position sets the framework for its study of psychology.

The task of behavioral psychology is to learn the laws of behavior. These laws are the same for all animals. A scientist can therefore discover many of the laws of human learning by studying the behavior of less complex creatures, such as rats and pigeons. Scientists, likewise, can refine the techniques of teaching through experimentation with animals. These techniques can then be applied to human beings.

*Education is a process of behavioral engineering.* From the behaviorist perspective, people are programmed to act in certain ways by their environment. They are rewarded for acting some ways and are punished for acting in other ways. Those activities that receive a positive reward tend to be repeated, while those receiving a negative reward tend to be extinguished. This process of positive and negative reward (reinforcement) shapes or programs a person to behave in certain ways. Behavior may be modified, therefore, by manipulating environmental reinforcers. The task of education is to create learning environments that lead to desired behaviors. Schooling and other educative institutions are therefore viewed as ways of designing a culture.

Skinner and other behaviorists claim that environmental conditioning and programming have always been a part of education and schooling. What they are calling for is a more con-

---

[36] Ibid., p. 24.

scious use of the laws of learning to control individuals so that the quality of life and the chances of racial survival will be enhanced.[37]

*The teacher's role is to create an effective learning environment.* Skinner and other behaviorists have, over the years, advocated a thorough revision of classroom practices. The main ingredient missing in most school environments, claims Skinner, is positive reinforcement. Traditional education has tended to use aversive forms of control, such as corporal punishment, scolding, extra homework, forced labor, the withdrawal of privileges, and examinations designed to show what students do not know. Consequently, students, if they are to be positively reinforced, must learn ways of escaping from the aversive situation of the classroom through such techniques as daydreaming, becoming aggressive, or eventually dropping out of school.

Skinner's contention is that students learn in daily life through the consequences of their acts. The task of the teacher is to arrange a learning environment that will provide positive reinforcement for desired student actions. The unrewarded acts, in a controlled environment, will become extinguished over time.

Harold Ozmon and Sam Craver have summarized the basic procedures for behavior modification in the ordinary classroom in the following way:

> (1) Specify the desired outcome, what needs to be changed, and how it will be evaluated; (2) establish a favorable environment by removing unfavorable stimuli which might complicate learning; (3) choose the proper reinforcers for desired behavioral manifestations; (4) begin shaping desired behavior by utilizing immediate reinforcers for desired behavior; (5) once a pattern of desired behaviors has been begun, slacken the number

---

[37] Critics of behaviorism have no doubt regarding the power of behavioral engineering. They recognize that as long as people live on the animal level, they can be controlled by behavioral techniques. The point of difference between the behaviorists and some of the other educational theorists is whether or not people have the possibility of rising above the animal level. Behaviorism's critics are also concerned with the issue of who will control the environmental controllers.

of times reinforcers are given; (6) evaluate results and reassess for future development.[38]

It can be seen from the above summary that behavioral objectives and the proper use of positive reinforcers are central to the effective learning environment as set forth by behaviorists. To aid the teacher in the complex task of maintaining a rewarding environment, Skinner and others have advocated programmed textbooks and other materials that break up the subject matter into small steps so that students will be rewarded positively as they complete each step successfully. Reinforcement occurs frequently because the successive steps in the learning process are as small as possible. Teaching machines have been advocated by behaviorists to aid in this process of sequential learning.

*Efficiency, economy, precision, and objectivity are central value considerations in education.* These values are fostered by both the philosophic orientation of behaviorism and by the objectives of the business community with which the school coexists in modern culture. Behavioral techniques have been applied to such business practices as systems management, advertising, and sales promotion with a great deal of success. This has led a large sector of the business community to join the psychological behaviorists in calling for schools and individual educators to be "accountable." The accountability movement has sought to fix the responsibility for instructional outcomes—what children learn—upon those doing the teaching. That mindset has stimulated an interest in applying business management techniques, objectives, and performance-based measures to school contexts.

It has been felt by the critics of behaviorism that its whole approach to education is based on a simplistic notion of the educative process and a false premise that equates training and manipulation with education. They suggest that what may be successful as an advertising technique may not be sufficient for the education of children.

---

[38]Howard Ozmon and Sam Craver, *Philosophical Foundations of Education* (Columbus, Ohio: Charles E. Merrill Publishing Co., 1976), p. 149.

# Educational Anarchism:
# The Deschooling Proposal[39]

By 1970 the Western world had witnessed some 2,500 years of periodic attempts at educational reform and 150 years of intensified reform as schooling became available to the masses. The year 1970 saw a proposal that went beyond educational reform to the realm of educational revolution. This movement was initiated by the publication of *Deschooling Society* by Ivan Illich. Illich's approach to the social order is basically that of anti-institutionalism and disestablishment. He opposed institutionalism on the grounds that it monopolized services and opportunities and set rigid and expensive routes as the only way of fulfilling basic human needs.

Illich saw the school system as the archenemy of his vision of the good life, since it taught all youth to look to the institutional model as the ideal.

> The pupil is thereby "schooled" to confuse teaching with learning, grade advancement with education, a diploma with competence, and fluency with the ability to say something new. His imagination is "schooled" to accept service in place of value. Medical treatment is mistaken for health care, social work for the improvement of community life, police protection for safety, military poise for national security, the rat race for productive work.[40]

---

[39] I am indebted to William F. O'Neill for the "educational anarchism" label. "Anarchism," he writes, "is the point of view that advocates the abolition of virtually all institutional restraints over human freedom as a way of providing the fullest expression of liberated human potentialities." (*Educational Ideologies: Contemporary Expressions of Educational Philosophy* [Santa Monica, Calif.: Goodyear Publishing Co., 1981], p. 287).

Anarchists, contending that external government is the root of evil, argue that harmony will prevail if external controls are abolished. Thus O'Neill's phrase aptly fits Illich's deschooling proposal.

[40] Ivan Illich, *Deschooling Society* (New York: Harper & Row, 1970), p. 1. See also, Ivan Illich et al, *After Deschooling What?* (New York: Harper & Row, Perennial Library, 1973), which critiques the deschooling proposal from a number of viewpoints.

The deschooling proposal calls for the disestablishment of the school and the repeal of compulsory education laws. In their place, Illich and his colleagues suggest a system of vouchers or tuition grants by which educational funds will be channeled directly to the beneficiaries, who will decide how to spend their funds in an attempt to buy their share of the education of their choice.

A good educational system, according to Illich,

> should have three purposes: it should provide all who want to learn with access to available resources at any time in their lives; empower all who want to share what they know to find those who want to learn it from them; and, finally, furnish all who want to present an issue to the public with the opportunity to make their challenge known.[41]

To help people become educated in a deschooled society, Illich recommends what he calls four "learning webs," or "educational networks," that would put learners in touch with teachers, other learners, and learning tools. He identifies these networks as reference services to educational objects, skill exchanges, peer-matching, and reference services to educators-at-large.[42]

Illich and his colleagues see the deschooling proposal as the answer to society's educational problems and social injustices. The critics of the proposal tend to see it as a pipe dream and Illich as a mystic.

## Perspective

The educational theories discussed in this chapter differ from the philosophies studied in chapters III and IV in the sense that the theories have been stimulated by educational problems rather than philosophic issues. The theorists, therefore, have not

[41] Ibid., p. 75.

[42] Ibid., pp. 76-79.

communicated to us in the language of philosophy, even though their theories have been built upon metaphysical, epistemological, and axiological beliefs. Part of the function of the study of educational philosophy is to heighten the awareness of educators concerning the philosophic assumptions undergirding the educational theories and to provide educators with the conceptual tools to evaluate those theories.

The contemporary educational theories have changed the shape of twentieth-century education. It is at the level of these theories that the educational battle has been, and is being, fought, both in the literature and in the schools. The theories have generated widespread educational experimentation and a literature aimed at both popular and professional audiences. Central to the struggle among the theorists has been the progressive position. Alfred North Whitehead once noted that all philosophy was actually a footnote to Plato—philosophers either aligned in some way with Plato or revolted against him. The same sort of statement might be made about educational theories in the twentieth century. Progressivism has served as a stimulus and a catalyst for both those who agree and those who disagree with its basic presuppositions and educational practices. That catalyst has instigated the formulation of contemporary theories in an era in which educational disputes have broken out of the cloistered realm of academia and into the public press. The vital issues faced by the theorists have enlisted both interest and enthusiasm for educational ideas and experimentation among large sectors of the reading public.

123

# ANALYTIC PHILOSOPHY AND EDUCATION

# 6

## The Analytic Movement in Philosophy

**A**nalytic philosophy might best be seen as a revolt against the traditional aims and methods of philosophy. It is not a school of philosophy, but rather an approach to doing philosophy. In the twentieth century this approach has dominated much of the philosophical work in English-speaking countries. As a result, many educational philosophers in both the United States and Great Britain deal with philosophic and educational issues from the analytic position. It is therefore imperative that students of educational philosophy become acquainted with the analytic rationale and methodology if they are to have a basic understanding of the field.

The analytic movement in philosophy, unlike such outlooks as idealism and pragmatism, is not a systematic philosophy. It is not interested in making metaphysical, epistemological, or axiological statements. On the contrary, it is quite convinced that the broad, sweeping statements of philosophers have merely added to the confusion of mankind. The problems of the past, claim the analysts, were not really problems concerning ultimate reality, truth, and value, but problems having to do with confusion in language and meaning. Imprecision in the use of language and unclear meanings stand at the center of philosophic confusion.

Many of our philosophic problems find their genesis in the "sloppy" use of language.

Analytic philosophers, therefore, turn away from the speculative, prescriptive, and synthesizing roles of philosophy. They refuse to develop philosophic theories.[1] The common denominator of the analysts, who have some serious disagreements among themselves, is the logical criticism of language and the way language can be misleading. Their unifying theme might be seen in the term "clarification." The goal of analytic philosophy has been succinctly described by Ludwig Wittgenstein:

> Philosophy aims at the logical clarification of thoughts.
> Philosophy is not a body of doctrine but an activity.
> A philosophical work consists essentially of elucidations.
> Philosophy does not result in "philosophical propositions," but rather in the clarification of propositions.
> Without philosophy thoughts are, as it were, cloudy and indistinct: its task is to make them clear and to give them sharp boundaries.[2]

Genuine knowledge, claim most analysts, is the business of science rather than philosophy. The true role of philosophy is critical clarification.

In one sense, analytic philosophy has a history that reaches back to the Greeks. Certainly Socrates was concerned that terms and concepts be properly understood, and Aristotle took an interest in precisely defining the words he used. On the other hand, the movement is a phenomenon of the twentieth century. Perhaps the difference between the twentieth-century model and the use of analysis in the past might best be seen in terms of means and ends. For philosophers prior to the twentieth century,

---

[1] The reason analytic philosophy has been treated in isolation from the traditional and modern philosophies in this text is that the analysts have separated themselves from the perennial concerns of philosophy by focusing on analysis rather than on the full range of philosophic activity. The separation in this chapter, therefore, is not artificial, but inherent in the world of philosophy itself.

[2] Ludwig Wittgenstein, *Tractatus Logico-Philosophicus*, trans. D. F. Pears and B. F. McGuinness (London: Routledge and Kegan Paul, 1961), p. 49 (4.112).

125

analysis was a means of clarifying language, so that the implications of their philosophic propositions might be understood. They were most concerned with the precise use of language in order that they might achieve the end of making meaningful statements about reality and truth. The analytic philosopher, by way of contrast, sees the precise use of language (as far as philosophy is concerned) as an end in itself. He does not make propositions, but is rather interested in clarifying the exact meaning of the propositions set down by others.

The historical roots of modern philosophic analysis can be traced back to linguistic analysis and positivism. Linguistic analysis developed in early twentieth-century England. It was stimulated by Bertrand Russell and Alfred North Whitehead's *Principia Mathematica*, which was published in three volumes between 1910 and 1914. Russell and Whitehead reduced mathematics to a logical language. Their idea was that mathematics possessed a clarity and logic that was, unfortunately, not found in the general use of language. George Edward Moore, another Englishman, took a different tack from Whitehead and Russell in claiming that the analysis of ordinary language and common sense, rather than scientific-mathematical language, should be the focal point of linguistic analysis. Perhaps the person who made the largest impact on the analytic movement was Ludwig Wittgenstein, who published his *Tractatus Logico-Philosophicus* in the early twenties. Wittgenstein, in his early years, was influenced by Russell, his teacher; and his work, in turn, influenced the positivistic philosophers of the Vienna Circle.

A second major root of modern philosophic analysis was positivism. The nineteenth-century French positivists, under the lead of Auguste Comte, held the position that knowledge must be based on sense perceptions and the investigations of objective science. Positivism, therefore, limited knowledge to statements of observable facts and their interrelations, and rejected metaphysical world views or world views that contained elements that could not be empirically verified. This negative attitude toward any reality beyond the human senses has influenced many modern fields of thought, including pragmatism, behaviorism, scientific naturalism, and the analytic movement. Positivism became the rallying point for a group of twentieth-century scholars known as the Vienna Circle. This group was made up largely of scientists, mathematicians, and symbolic logicians who were interested in philosophy. The Vienna Circle saw philosophy as the logic of science, and their thought form came to be known as logical positivism. A major aim of this group was to find an inclusive terminological and conceptual system common to all the sciences. This led them away from a possible role of criticizing the arguments of traditional philosophy, and toward the study of the language of particular sciences and an analysis of language in general in the hope of finding a universal language of science. Positivists of all varieties have put a great deal of stock in the assumption that human observers can achieve neutrality in their investigations. As noted previously, they also uplifted the principle of rigorous empirical verification. A crucial weakness in their position developed when, in their zeal for verification, they ruled out any consideration of unverifiable propositions. It was in time realized, to the discomfort and depreciation of positivism, that some of the fundamental assumptions of science itself were unverifiable in the way verification was applied by the positivists.

It should be noted that analytic philosophy is an umbrella term that encompasses a number of somewhat diverse viewpoints that are referred to under such labels as logical positivism, logical empiricism, linguistic analysis, logical atomism, and Oxford analysis.

## The Role of Philosophic
## Analysis in Education

At this point, it should be clear that the role of analytic philosophy in regard to education is radically different from the relationship between the philosophic "schools" and the educational enterprise. "There was a time," notes R. S. Peters, a leading analytic philosopher, "when it was taken for granted that the philosophy of education consisted in the formulation of high-level directives which would guide educational practice and

127

shape the organization of schools."[3] In other words, the function of educational philosophy has traditionally been (and has been put forth in this book) to develop and prescribe educational aims and practices that are built upon, and are in harmony with, a philosophic outlook based on a particular view concerning the nature of reality, truth, and value. That approach obviously runs into conflict with the stance of Wittgenstein, who in his early career stated that metaphysical statements are "nonsense."

What then, we might ask, are the value, use, and function of educational philosophy for the analyst? The answer is given to us by Peters, who says that one of the main preoccupations of the analytic philosopher is to lay "high-level directives for education . . . under the analytic guillotine."[4] In essence, Peters and his colleagues are stating that the role of educational philosophy is not to develop some new educational "ism" or ideology, but to help us better understand the meanings of our current ideologies. The benefit to be achieved for students, parents, teachers, administrators, and society from such a clarification will be a more meaningful approach to the educational process. Analysts contend that many educational problems are essentially language problems. Therefore, if we can solve the language problems, then we can better disentangle the educational problems.

One charge of the analysts is that many educational statements are nonsense. Samuel Shermis has illustrated this point, as well as analytic methodology, by a simple example.

> Analysts might give attention to such typical statements as, "Teachers should provide real-life experiences for their students" or "The curriculum should be based on lifelike situations." First, these statements should be recognized as prescriptions, statements of what someone ought to do, rather than descriptions. Second, the descriptive terms "real-life experience" and "lifelike" should be examined to determine their meanings. The term "life" is a description of all the activities of human beings. One

[3] R. S. Peters, *Ethics and Education* (London: George Allen & Unwin, 1966), p. 15.

[4] Ibid.

of the activities of living human beings is conjugating verbs. Yet as this statement is usually employed, conjugating verbs is not what is meant, for grammatical exercises are not considered "lifelike." But if grammar is part of "life," why should it not be included in the prescription?[5]

According to Shermis, the type of statements in the above quotation are examples of the all-too-common substitution of ambiguous emotive slogans for meaningful, precise terms. Education, unfortunately, is riddled with imprecise statements and slogans, and analytic philosophers perform a valuable service in their function as clarifiers of language, concepts, and purposes.

It should be seen from the above illustration that the use of analysis can dissolve some problems through the act of clarification by demonstrating that certain statements or prescriptions are meaningless, or at least misleading, as they are stated. In a certain sense, that is a negative function. On the other hand, dissolving issues that are pseudo problems is an important service if teachers are to have time to deal with meaningful concerns. "To the extent that teachers need not worry about doing the impossible—in this case 'providing lifelike' experiences—to that extent can they ask themselves questions which really make sense."[6]

The simplicity of the above example should not be taken as being typical of analytic procedure. It was chosen specifically for its brevity and simplicity. The "doing" or reading of analytic philosophy is a rigorous, exacting, and tedious business that would tend to bore most people quite rapidly. That may be seen by some as a disadvantage, but not to the analytic philosopher, who claims that no progress has ever come in the scientific and mathematical realms without a great deal of rigorous effort and precision; those are prerequisites to progress.

Philosophical analysts are not only interested in clarifying the educator's use of language, but also in clarifying the

[5] S. Samuel Shermis, *Philosophic Foundations of Education* (New York: D. Van Nostrand Company, 1967). p. 266.

[6] Ibid., p. 267.

conceptual devices used by the educator, the processes of using them, their underlying presuppositions, and the purposes involved. A typical introductory textbook in educational philosophy from the analytic position centers around an analysis of the "concept of education," the "concept of training, " the "concept of child-centered," and other concepts including, "aims," "culture," "curriculum," "liberal education," "conditioning and indoctrination," "value-judgment," "values," "morals," and "freedom and authority."[7] With the exception of the introductory chapter, this listing exhausts the table of contents for a three-hundred-page book. The above list of contents is given in the hope that the reader will intuit the difference between the approach taken by an analytic introduction to educational philosophy and the survey-type approach utilized by *Issues and Alternatives* and many other nonanalytic introductions.

Analysts not only avoid making prescriptive statements about what students and teachers ought to do or ought not to do, but they also avoid statements of value concerning such activities. For example, let us suppose that the suggestion is put forth by certain school authorities that elementary students should read the Macmillan Basal Readers up through the sixth grade. The function of the analyst, in this case, would not be to attempt to say whether a child should read Macmillan or something else, but to examine the claims made regarding the merits of such activities. Instead of saying that a child should read, think, or learn, the analyst will examine what is meant by "read," "think," or "learn," and will not prescribe nor make a value judgment; his or her function is to clarify through analysis.

One area into which the analysts have moved in education is the development of models which help us clarify and order our concepts. These models might be thought of in terms of strategies to help us in specific "language games." Analysts have also developed theoretical models to help teachers with particular problems. They note that scientists often construct a theoretical model before engaging in an activity. It follows, claim the analysts, that

[7] Harry Schofield, *The Philosophy of Education: An Introduction* (London: George Allen & Unwin, 1972).

the same would be helpful in teaching. The use of models can help clear up ambiguity and can thereby aid the profession.

## Evaluation of Analytic Philosophy

Philosophic analysis has in many ways improved educational philosophy by making it more sensitive to the implications of educational terms and adding rigor and precision to the study of education as a professional field. The analytic critique of education has brought about an awareness and a critical attitude that should help the profession be wary of ready-made answers, slogans, and clichés as solutions to social and educational dilemmas. Clarification of educational ideas and statements has been needed in the past, and will be just as needed in the future if professional education is to make progress rather than being content merely with ill-defined motion.

On the other hand, analytic philosophy as an educational philosophy has some glaring weaknesses if analysis is seen as the *only* meaningful way of doing philosophy. First, there is a widespread criticism that philosophic analysis is too narrow and too limited to meet adequately the complex demands of modern life, society, and education. Abraham Kaplan, speaking to this point, has written:

> But note how great is the preoccupation here with purely intellectual goals and standards—the emphasis is on science, truth, belief, observation, and inference. But art, beauty, morality, politics, and religion apparently lie outside the scope of this powerful method, if not outside the scope of philosophical interest altogether. . . . I cannot help but feel that there is something seriously wrong with a philosophy, in the mid-twentieth century, that takes no notice of war, revolution, nationalism, nuclear energy, the exploration of space, or anything else distinctive of the life of our time save the magnificient sweep of the intellect in the achievements of pure science and mathematics.[8]

[8] Abraham Kaplan, *The New World of Philosophy* (New York: Random House, 1961), pp. 89-90.

Philosophic analysis, in its attempts to achieve clarity and precision, has been seen by some as an escape from the really important problems of this century and the perennial issues of philosophy.

A second criticism of analytic philosophy is that it is prone to confuse philosophic means with philosophic ends. In its search for clarification and precision, it often has glorified philosophic techniques, and, to a certain extent, turned the philosopher into a highly-skilled technician. One might seriously ask the analytic philosopher not only where we are to go after we have cleared up our ambiguities, but whether clarification of what we are doing is of much value if we are doing the wrong things at the outset. One analytic philosopher, sensing this problem, has noted that perhaps "a certain systemic ambiguity is more desirable than an artificial precision."[9] Kaplan also warns us to beware of the implications of any trade-offs made between gains in philosophic precision and losses in philosophic wisdom.[10] In regard to the confusion of ends and means, John Wild has noted that the person who is confused on this point "is like a man who becomes so interested in the cracks and spots of dust upon his glasses that he loses all interest in what he may actually see through them."[11] Analytic philosophy, if seen as the only mode of doing philosophy, could develop into "little more than a new form of scholasticism where, instead of arguing about how many angels can stand on the head of a pin, they debate how the words 'should' and 'ought' may be used."[12] We must realize that even if philosophers cease to speak on metaphysical and axiological questions, others, such as social and physical scientists, will continue to make grand statements and propositions in regard to life and education. One cannot escape facing mankind's basic questions

[9] Jonas F. Soltis, *An Introduction to the Analysis of Educational Concepts*, 2d ed. (Reading, Mass.: Addison-Wesley Publishing Co., 1978), p. 82. This is an excellent introduction to analytic method.

[10] Kaplan, *The New World of Philosophy*, p. 58.

[11] John Wild, *The Challenge of Existentialism* (Bloomington, Ind.: Indiana Univ. Press, 1955), p. 10.

[12] Ozmon and Craver, *Philosophical Foundations of Education*, p. 216.

by merely defining them in such a way that they fall outside the definition of philosophy. If philosophers do not do philosophy, then someone else will. Philosophy in its "grand manner" will continue, and educational prescriptions will therefore continue to be made, with or without the aid of professional philosophers. A myopic confusion of ends and means leads nowhere beyond the ideal of clarification of propositions for the sake of clarification. That is a negative rather than a positive philosophic position.

A third criticism of analytic philosophy as a total way of approaching philosophic issues stems from its seeming blindness to its own metaphysical and epistemological presuppositions. On the one hand, analysts generally eschew *a priori* assumptions. On the other hand, when they insist that every descriptive or factual term must be in the language of science and that propositions must be verifiable by sensory observation, they assume a metaphysical doctrine in harmony with materialism, realism, and positivism. As such, their metaphysics and epistemology, whether consciously or unconsciously selected, are open to the same criticisms as those philosophic positions.

## The Complementary Roles of Analytic and Synoptic Philosophy

Not all analytic philosophers have taken a position that identifies analytic philosophy with the total task of philosophy. Many leading analysts realize that they have chosen to specialize in one mode of doing philosophy and that there are other modes that can answer different sorts of questions than those asked by analytic philosophy.[13] Unfortunately, many proponents (especially early advocates) of analytic philosophy have not always espoused that balance.

Perhaps the best way to look at the relationship between the synoptic and analytic ways of doing philosophy might be to see

[13] Frederick Copleston, *Contemporary Philosophy: Studies of Logical Positivism and Existentialism*, rev. ed. (London: Search Press, 1972), chap. 1.

them in terms of being complementary to one another. Jonas F. Soltis, an analyst, has noted that possibly the phrase "in tandem" could express the relationship between analytic and world-view philosophies.[14] In this relationship the techniques of analysis could be used to clarify and make more precise and intelligible the broad and comprehensive concepts of synoptic philosophical systems.[15] Soltis illustrates this "in tandem" idea through analogy:

> If we could liken the use of analysis to the use of a microscope (and some also use this instrument well or poorly), then we might also liken the traditional philosophical world-view building to the astronomer's use of the telescope in charting the universe. The instruments are designed for different tasks, and so we should expect different results from their respective uses. But the fruitful use of one does not preclude or deny the validity of the use of the other; nor does it cancel the possibility that they may be used in conjunction or in some other complementary way. Thus I would argue that, although there are certain limits to philosophical analysis, these limits are not as narrow and circumscribed as some contemporary philosophers of education believe. In a word, these two approaches are not necessarily antithetical and can complement each other in the unending philosophical attempt to better conceptualize and understand the complex process of education from every available vantage point.[16]

## Perspective

In conclusion, it may be noted that analytic philosophy, by itself, is incomplete. Certain analytic philosophers may have

---

[14] Soltis, *An Introduction to the Analysis of Educational Concepts*, p. 82.

[15] I would suggest that this same basic relationship should hold between statistical and documentary research in education—a point at which we at times experience some confusion and hard feelings both within departments and in the academic community at large.

[16] Soltis, *An Introduction to the Analysis of Educational Concepts*, p. 83.

turned away from the broader concerns of philosophy, but they have not invalidated those concerns. Someone must still make speculative decisions concerning such issues as the nature and destiny of mankind and the nature of truth if civilized life is to continue. Out of these decisions will proceed prescriptions in regard to society and its schools. Humanity must still have visions of the good life; and, as a result, the fourfold role of philosophy in its synthetic, speculative, prescriptive, and analytic aspects must be integrated. No one function may become the whole of philosophy without distorting the entire quest for answers to mankind's basic questions.

The weaknesses of analytic philosophy as the only mode of doing philosophy are quite obvious. On the other hand, educators have much to learn from the analytic movement. For example, much of the language and many of the concepts used by educators are unnecessarily imprecise. In addition, there are many emotive slogans and ambiguities that have led to semantic difficulties in educational thought and communication. The insights and methods of the analysts are needed for building a philosophy of education. These insights and methods, however, should not be seen as an end in themselves or as a complete approach to philosophy, but rather as a philosophic activity that helps educators sharpen the speculative, prescriptive, and synthetic aspects of their philosophic enterprise.

# TOWARD A PERSONAL PHILOSOPHY OF EDUCATION

# 7

**T**hus far in our study of educational philosophy we have surveyed the basic issues and alternatives that are important to the practicing educator. Chapters I and II highlighted the role of philosophy in education, analyzed the basic issues of philosophy, and noted the relationship of philosophic issues to educational goals and practice. Chapters III through VI examined the various answers that traditional and modern philosophers have given to the basic questions of philosophy, pointed out some of the implications of their answers for educational practice, and discussed the theories of education that have been the focal point of much of the educational ferment of the twentieth century.

This chapter will briefly treat the relationship of these issues and alternatives to the individual educator. It will then discuss the need for a personal philosophy, some processes for developing a philosophy, and some of the challenges involved in implementing that philosophy.

## The Need for a Personal Philosophy of Education

Each of us has a philosophy of life that we carry into the classroom. We have, for example, convictions about the world, the meaning of life, and what is ethically right. We have, furthermore, a philosophy of education with which we operate every day. For instance, when teachers administer and grade examinations for the purpose of encouraging students to master material, they are not merely attempting to measure knowledge. Such an action implies a belief in regard to human nature—that students really won't put forth the effort needed to master the field unless teachers provide a sufficiently powerful incentive (i.e., most students tend to laziness in intellectual matters). Our daily actions in the school are fraught with deeper meanings than lie on the surface. Why do we act the way we do in the classroom, rather than some other way? There must be a reason, or else we wouldn't do the same things term after term. Our actions are rooted in our philosophy.

To say that each of us has a philosophy of education and life that we daily act upon does not mean that we have a good (or bad) philosophy, or even a philosophy that we have thought through. Our philosophy may lie at the subliminal level. The plea of this chapter is that all educators need a *consciously examined* and *thoroughly considered* philosophy of education if they are to make the most efficient use of both their own time and their students' energy.

Too often educators operate out of their philosophic "hip pocket"—they act without having thought about why they act. As a result, they frequently do not achieve as much as they could, even though they may have had a "successful" day. It is difficult to arrive at our goal if we do not know the steps that need to be taken to get there. It is equally difficult to decide upon the necessary steps if we are unsure about our goal or destination. A well thought-out philosophy should help even good teachers become better. We must first clearly see what we are seeking to achieve, then we can bend our energies toward reaching our goal.

On the first page of this book, it was noted that one of the most pertinent criticisms of American education is its "mindlessness." Education has suffered from too much motion without sufficient thought about purposes, goals, and actual needs. What is it that you, as an individual educator, really hope to

137

accomplish? Why are you teaching math, biology, or American literature? Is it worth the trouble? If so, what difference should it make in the lives of your students and the society in which they live?

Samuel Shermis has perceptively noted that "all educational issues are ultimately philosophical." More money and better equipment will not in themselves solve the problems in current education. What is needed are parents, teachers, administrators, school board members, curriculum developers, and other decision-makers who understand the issues at their deepest level.[1] With understanding comes, at least, the possibility of success. Without understanding, education is doomed to futility.

You as an educator need a consciously considered and well-thought-out philosophy, because it will (1) help you understand the most basic problems of education, (2) enable you to evaluate better the wide variety of suggestions offered as solutions to these problems, (3) assist you in clarifying your thinking about the goals of life and education, and (4) guide you in the development of an internally consistent point of view and a program that relates realistically to the larger world context.

# Developing a Personal
# Philosophy of Education

After being introduced to the six philosophies and eight educational theories covered in this book, you may well feel yourself inundated with "isms." A first thought might be that the purpose of studying educational philosophy is to get you to choose and practice the educational implications of one of the "isms." Wrong! The purpose of studying educational philosophy is rather to present students with the basic philosophic issues and the most significant educational alternatives, so that they will better be able to think about education and evaluate suggestions for intelligent action.

[1] Shermis, *Philosophic Foundations of Education*, p. 277.

Knowing the systematic "isms" is not the end of philosophic understanding. This knowledge is really closer to the beginning. The philosophers of old (and late) never saw themselves primarily as builders of systems of thought. Rather, they were seeking to solve life's problems in an integrated and nonconflicting manner. Likewise, as a student of educational philosophy, you are under no obligation to accept or develop a "system" of philosophy. But you do have a major obligation to consciously think through what you are doing and why you are doing it. The actions of educators, after all, affect human lives. It is irresponsible for educators to have unexamined world views. The commitment that all educators must have is twofold: first, to think through the issues and alternatives of educational philosophy in the belief that intelligent thought can improve success; and, second, to put the fruitage of that thought at the foundation of their professional and personal lives. What is needed is not a "philosophic blueprint," but a heightened sensitivity to the challenges of professional responsibility.

After realizing that accepting an "ism" is not an expected result of a course in educational philosophy, you might conclude that the correct line of action is to pick and choose the "best" and "most useful" from each of the theories and philosophies—to become an eclectic. This alternative is undoubtedly encouraged by the realization that each of the "isms" has captured at least part of the truth about mankind, education, and society.

While eclecticism may be tempting to the beginner (and may even be a necessary starting point in some cases), it is generally an inadequate base for satisfactory educational practice. With the passage of time and with added conceptual maturity comes the realization that eclecticism is nearly always only a "second best" method of developing an educational position. It soon becomes apparent, for instance, that eclecticism may lead to internal contradictions as a person selects a bit from this philosophy and a piece from that theory. The maturing educator is also bound to realize, sooner or later, that two different philosophic schools can use the same words while implying different meanings, and that they can suggest what are apparently the same methodologies to bring about dissimilar results, since they have different starting points, goals, and directions.

The most basic problem of eclecticism, however, is the fact that it reflects an underlying system of values on the part of the eclectic. For example, the careful reader may have noted that the above discussion used the terms "best" and "most useful" in discussing the basis of eclectic choice. The very use of these words implies that eclectics have a philosophical base with a definite axiology that they use to make value judgments. The task for educators is to come to grips with the basic presuppositions that in reality undergird their surface eclecticism. This task points beyond eclecticism to an examination of one's underlying world view. John Brubacher has noted that an eclectic philosophy may not be an impossible position for the uncritical thinker, but "it is difficult to justify on close examination."[2] It is better to develop a personal philosophy of education.

There are at least two ways in which you, as an individual, can come to grips with your philosophy of education. The first is for you to examine, in the light of the discussion in chapter II, your most basic convictions concerning reality, truth, and value. Once you have consciously thought through these philosophic issues and developed a view, then you are in a position to make some statements in regard to what you believe the goals of education in general should be. In addition, you will be able to outline some of your personal goals as a teacher of a certain subject at a particular grade level in a specific school setting. With your philosophic framework and educational goals in mind, you will be in a position to make specific assertions about the meaning of your philosophy for educational practice in terms of your work with students, your role as a teacher, your curricular priorities, and your preferred teaching methods. Once this is done, you are ready to put your developing theory into practice with the full realization that classroom experience will tend to modify your theoretical framework as you broaden the range of your

---

[2] Brubacher, *Modern Philosophies of Education*, pp. 134-35.

understanding. This approach to philosophy building is the one most emphasized in this textbook.[3]

A second approach to building a philosophy is what Van Cleve Morris calls the inductive method.[4] According to this method, you should start with your own teaching experience. First, examine what you do in your teaching behavior, especially noting those behaviors that are most successful. Then, on the basis of your knowledge of the philosophies and educational theories, attempt to specify the theoretical framework which you relate to most closely and the metaphysical, epistemological, and axiological perspectives upon which you seem to be operating. Next, seek to refine your philosophy in relation to your practice, and vice versa, until you have developed a consistent approach to your profession.

In conclusion, it should be realized that whether you begin with philosophy and logically deduce practices, begin with practice and induce your philosophy, or develop your philosophy in some other way, you still have an obligation to yourself, your students, and the community you serve to do the very best you can as an educator. It is implicit in the rationale for teaching educational philosophy that the best job is more closely correlated to intelligent action than to ignorance. The educator is therefore under obligation to develop and act upon a well-considered philosophy of education.

## Implementing a Personal Philosophy of Education

A well-thought-out philosophy of education has value only if it is a means to an end, rather than being an end in itself. That end should be more successful educational practice. Students too often think of the study of educational philosophy as a relatively useless game of mental gymnastics. On the contrary, educational philosophy, if its purpose is really understood, is the most

[3] E.g., pp. 34-36.

[4] Van Cleve Morris, *Philosophy and the American School*, pp. 464-65.

practical of all subjects in the training of educators. Without educational philosophy there can be no meaningful practice. A first step in improving practice is, therefore, a sound attempt to improve our thinking about what we are doing and why we are doing it.

As important as educational philosophy is, however, every educator must realize that it is only one of several foundational elements that undergird the educational process. While philosophy provides the basic boundaries for the preferred educative practices for any group in society, other factors, including the political climate, economic conditions, the needs of the labor market, and the social conceptions of a specific population, certainly impact upon educational practice. Educational decisions are made in a dynamic milieu in which many factors contend for recognition. As a professional in education, you must make responsible, intelligent choices in relation to your particular social context. In the calculus used in the decision-making process, educational philosophy is a major, rather than the only, factor that must be considered. The professional training of educators should therefore contain significant introductions to sociological, historical, psychological, political, and economic foundations of education, as well as a solid introduction to educational philosophy.

In implementing your personal philosophy of education, you must come to grips with the possibility that your philosophy and the philosophy of the district for which you teach may not be in complete harmony. That is particularly true in a modern pluralistic society like the United States. The ideal, of course, is that your individual philosophy and that of your employing school district will be congruent. Many educators, however, will have to decide how to be faithful to the goals of their employer, while at the same time being honest to their personal convictions. That is not always an easy task, but neither is it impossible. One helpful reality is that pluralistic societies provide a fairly wide spectrum of philosophic tolerance. This allows for differing individuals to set forth varying viewpoints within a rather loose consensus of accepted "essentials." On the other hand, there are justifiable limits to philosophic tolerance in educational settings. American high schools, for example, can hardly be expected to employ openly active revolutionary communists as political-science instructors.

Aside from such extreme cases, American teachers have a remarkable amount of freedom to operate within the context of their personal convictions. With this freedom, however, comes the obligation of responsible classroom performance.

In most cases, understanding educators will be able to work within the context of the goals of the larger society, while still being true to their personal beliefs. One of the purposes for studying educational philosophy is to provide you with tools for better understanding your personal philosophy, the social philosophy of the culture in which you live and work, and the means that you can utilize to responsibly blend the two.

In conclusion, it is important to realize that philosophy-building is an ongoing process. As an educator, you will continually gain new insights; and as your breadth of knowledge and practical experience expands, you will be constantly developing your philosophy. Educational professionals should think of educational philosophy as something they "do" on a perpetual basis, rather than as something they once studied in a course with those words in the title.

This is the end of this book, but it will hopefully be the beginning of your personal philosophy-building. The building of a personal philosophy for both life and education is a continuing process of thought and practice that becomes richer, deeper, and more meaningful as you develop professionally. The successful educator is a thinking educator. You must not pretend that you now understand philosophy and education and can therefore move on to more important things. Your philosophy is an integral part of who you are and everything you do. Your growth in this area, as well as in other areas of human endeavor, must be a dynamic and ongoing process.

# BIBLIOGRAPHY

Adler, Mortimer J. "In Defense of the Philosophy of Education." In *Philosophies of Education*. National Society for the Study of Education, Forty-first Yearbook, Part I. Chicago: University of Chicago Press, 1942.

Adler, Mortimer J. "The Crisis in Contemporary Education." *Social Frontier* 5 (February 1939): 144.

Adler, Mortimer J. *Paideia Problems and Possibilities*. New York: Macmillan Publishing Co., 1983.

Adler, Mortimer J., ed., *The Paideia Program: An Educational Syllabus*. New York: Macmillan Publishing Co., 1984.

Adler, Mortimer J. *The Paideia Proposal: An Educational Manifesto*. New York: Macmillan Publishing Co., 1982.

Aquinas, Thomas. *Summa Theologica*. 3 vols. Translated by Fathers of the English Dominican Province. New York: Benziger Bros., 1947.

Bestor, Arthur E. *Educational Wastelands: The Retreat from Learning in Our Public Schools*. Urbana, Ill.: The University of Illinois Press, 1953.

Bestor, Arthur E. *The Restoration of Learning: A Program for Redeeming the Unfulfilled Promise of American Education*. New York: Alfred A. Knopf, 1955.

Bloom, Allan. *The Closing of the American Mind*. New York: Simon & Schuster, 1987.

Brameld, Theodore. *Education as Power*. New York: Holt, Reinhart and Winston, 1965.

Brameld, Theodore. *Education for the Emerging Age*. New York: Harper & Row, 1961.

Brameld, Theodore. *Patterns of Educational Philosophy*. New York: Harcourt, Brace & World, 1950.

Brameld, Theodore. *Toward a Reconstructed Philosophy of Education*. New York: Holt, Rinehart and Winston, 1956.

Broudy, Harry S. *Building a Philosophy of Education.* 2d ed. Englewood Cliffs, N.J.: Prentice Hall, 1961.

Broudy, Harry S. *The Uses of Schooling.* New York: Routledge, 1988.

Broudy, Harry S. "What Schools Should and Should Not Teach," *Peabody Journal of Education,* October 1976, pp. 31-38.

Brubacher, John S. *Modern Philosophies of Education.* 4th ed. New York: McGraw-Hill Co., 1969.

Buber, Martin. *Between Man and Man.* London: Kegan Paul, 1947.

Butler, J. Donald. *Four Philosophies and Their Practice in Education and Religion.* 3d ed. New York: Harper & Row, 1968.

Butler, J. Donald. *Idealism in Education.* New York: Harper & Row, 1966.

Camus, Albert. *The Myth of Sisyphus and Other Essays.* Translated by Justin O'Brien. New York: Vintage Books, 1955.

Carper, James C., and Hunt, Thomas C., eds., *Religious Schooling in America.* Birmingham, Alabama: Religious Education Press, 1984.

Chapman, J. Crosby, and Counts, George S. *Principles of Education.* Boston: Houghton Mifflin Co., 1924.

Coleman, James S. et al. *Equality of Educational Opportunity.* Washington, D.C.: U.S. Department of Health, Education, and Welfare, 1966.

College Board, *Academic Preparation for College.* New York: The College Board, 1983.

Conant, James B. *The American High School Today.* New York: McGraw-Hill Book Co., 1959.

Copleston, Frederick. *Contemporary Philosophy: Studies of Logical Positivism and Existentialism.* Rev. ed. London: Search Press, 1972.

Counts, George S. *Dare the School Build a New Social Order?* New York: John Day Co., 1932.

Counts, George S. *Education and American Civilization.* New York: Teachers College, Columbia University, Bureau of Publications, 1952.

Counts, George S. *Education and the Foundations of Human Freedom.* Pittsburgh: University of Pittsburgh Press, 1962.

Counts, George S. *The Soviet Challenge to America.* New York: John Day Co., 1931.

Cremin, Lawrence A. *The Genius of American Education.* New York: Vintage Books, 1965.

Cremin, Lawrence A. *Public Education.* New York: Basic Books, 1976.

Cremin, Lawrence A. *The Transformation of the School: Progressivism in American Education, 1876-1957.* New York: Vintage Books, 1964.

Dennison, George. *The Lives of Children.* New York: Random House, 1969.

Dewey, John. *Art as Experience.* New York: Minton, Balch & Co. 1934.

Dewey, John. *Democracy and Education.* New York: The Macmillan Co., 1916.

Dewey, John. *Experience and Education.* New York: The Macmillan Co., 1938.

Dewey, John. *How We Think: A Restatement of the Relation of Reflective Thinking to the Educative Process.* New ed. New York: D. C. Heath and Co., 1933.

Dewey, John. *The School and Society.* Rev. ed. Chicago: University of Chicago Press, 1915.

Falwell, Jerry. *Listen, America!* Garden City, N.Y.: Doubleday & Co., 1980.

Frankl, Viktor E. *Man's Search for Meaning: An Introduction to Logotherapy.* New York: Washington Square Press, 1963.

Freire, Paulo. *Pedagogy of the Oppressed.* Translated by Myra Bergman Ramos. New York: Seabury Press, 1968.

Gardner, John W. *Self-Renewal: The Individual in the Innovative Society.* New York: Harper & Row, 1964.

Glasser, William. *Schools Without Failure.* New York: Harper & Row, Perennial Library, 1975.

Greene, Maxine. *Teacher as Stranger: Educational Philosophy for the Modern Age.* Belmont, Calif.: Wadsworth Publishing Co., 1973.

Gross, Beatrice, and Gross, Ronald, eds. *The Great School Debate: Which Way for American Education?* New York: Simon & Shuster, 1985.

Gutek, Gerald L. *Philosophical and Ideological Perspectives on Education.* Englewood Cliffs, N.J.: Prentice Hall, 1988.

Hilgard, Ernest R., and Bower, Gordon H. *Theories of Learning.* 3d ed. New York: Appleton-Century-Crofts, 1966.

Hocking, William Ernest. *Types of Philosophy.* 3d ed. New York: Charles Scribner's Sons, 1959.

Holt, John. *Freedom and Beyond.* New York: Dell Publishing Co., Laurel Edition, 1972.

Holt, John. *How Children Fail.* New York: Pitman Publishing Corp., 1964.

Horne, Herman Harrell. *The Democratic Philosophy of Education.* New York: The Macmillan Co., 1932.

Horne, Herman Harrell. "An Idealistic Philosophy of Education." In *Philosophies of Education.* National Society for the Study of Education, Forty-first Yearbook, Part I. Chicago: University of Chicago Press, 1942.

Hutchins, Robert M. *The Conflict in Education.* New York: Harper & Brothers, 1953.

Hutchins, Robert M. *The Higher Learning in America.* New Haven, Conn.: Yale University Press, 1936.

Hutchins, Robert M. *The Learning Society.* New York: New American Library, 1968.

146

Illich, Ivan. *Deschooling Society*. New York: Harper & Row, 1970.

James, William. *Essays in Pragmatism*. Edited by Alburey Castell. New York: Hafner Publishing Co., 1948.

James, William. *Pragmatism*. New York: Longmans, Green, and Co., 1907.

Jencks, Christopher et al. *Inequality: A Reassessment of the Effect of Family and Schooling in America*. New York: Harper & Row, 1972.

Kaplan, Abraham. *The New World of Philosophy*. New York: Random House, 1961.

Kaufmann, Walter. *Existentialism from Dostoevsky to Sartre*. Rev. ed. New York: New American Library, 1975.

Keniston, Kenneth et al. *All Our Children: The American Family under Pressure*. New York: Harcourt Brace Jovanovich, 1977.

Kneller, George F. *Existentialism and Education*. New York: John Wiley & Sons, 1958.

Kneller, George F. *Introduction to the Philosophy of Education*. 2d ed. New York: John Wiley & Sons, 1971.

Knight, George R. "The Transformation of Change and the Future Role of Education." *Philosophic Research and Analysis* 8 (Early Spring 1980): 10-11.

Kohl, Herbert R. *The Open Classroom: A Practical Guide to a New Way of Teaching*. New York: New York Review, 1969.

Kohl, Herbert R. *36 Children*. New York: New American Library, 1967.

Kozol, Jonathan. *Death at an Early Age*. Boston: Houghton Mifflin Co., 1967.

Kozol, Jonathan. *Free Schools*. Boston: Houghton Mifflin Co., 1972.

LaHaye, Tim. *The Battle for the Mind*. Old Tappan, N.J.: Fleming H. Revell, 1980.

Laska, John A. *Schooling and Education: Basic Concepts and Problems*. New York: D. Van Nostrand Co., 1976.

Lucas, Christopher J., ed. *Challenge and Choice in Contemporary Education: Six Major Ideological Perspectives*. New York: Macmillan Publishing Co., 1976.

Maritain, Jacques. *Education at the Crossroads*. New Haven, Conn.: Yale University Press, 1943.

Marler, Charles D. *Philosophy and Schooling*. Boston: Allyn and Bacon, 1975.

Martin, Wm. Oliver. *Realism in Education*. New York: Harper & Row, 1969.

Morris, Charles. *Varieties of Human Value*. Chicago: The University of Chicago Press, 1956.

Morris, Van Cleve. *Existentialism in Education: What it Means*. New York: Harper & Row, 1966.

Morris, Van Cleve. *Philosophy and the American School*. Boston: Houghton Mifflin Company, 1961.

Nash, Paul; Kazamias, Andreas M.; and Perkinson, Henry J. *The Educated Man: Studies in the History of Educational Thought*. New York: John Wiley & Sons, 1966.

Nash, Paul. *Models of Man: Explorations in the Western Educational Tradition*. New York: John Wiley & Sons, 1968.

National Commission on Excellence in Education. *A Nation at Risk: The Imperative for Educational Reform*. Washington, D.C.: U.S. Government Printing Office, 1983.

Neff, Frederick C. *Philosophy and American Education*. New York: The Center for Applied Research in Education, 1966.

Neill, A. S. *Summerhill: A Radical Approach to Child Rearing*. New York: Hart Publishing Co., 1960.

O'Neill, William F. *Educational Ideologies: Contemporary Expressions of Educational Philosophy*. Santa Monica, Calif.: Goodyear Publishing Co., 1981.

Ornstein, Allan C. *An Introduction to the Foundations of Education*. Chicago: Rand McNally College Publishing Co., 1977.

Ozmon, Howard, and Craver, Sam. *Philosophical Foundations of Education*. Columbus, Ohio: Charles E. Merrill Publishing Co., 1976.

Perkinson, Henry J. *The Imperfect Panacea: American Faith in Education, 1865-1976*. 2d ed. New York: Random House, 1977.

Peters, R. S. *Ethics and Education*. London: George Allen & Unwin, 1966.

Plato. *The Dialogues*. 4 vols. Translated by B. Jowett. New York: Charles Scribner's Sons, 1872.

Postman, Neil, and Weingartner, Charles. *The School Book: For People Who Want to Know What All the Hollering Is About*. New York: Dell Publishing Co., 1973.

Rich, John Martin. *Education and Human Values*. Reading, Mass.: Addison-Wesley Publishing Co., 1968.

Rogers, Carl R. *Freedom to Learn*. Columbus, Ohio: Charles E. Merrill Publishing Co., 1969.

Rogers, Carl R. *On Becoming a Person: A Therapist's View of Psychotherapy*. Boston: Houghton Mifflin Co., 1961.

Rousseau, Jean-Jacques. *Emile, or On Education*. Translated by Allan Bloom. New York: Basic Books, 1979.

Sartre, Jean-Paul. *Existentialism and Human Emotions*. New York: Philosophical Library, 1957.

Schofield, Harry. *The Philosophy of Education: An Introduction*. London: George Allen & Unwin, 1972.

Schumacher, E. F. *A Guide for the Perplexed*. New York: Harper & Row, 1977.

148

Schumacher, E. F. *Small Is Beautiful: Economics as if People Mattered.* New York: Harper & Row, 1973.

Shane, Harold G. *The Educational Significance of the Future.* Bloomington, Indiana: Phi Delta Kappa, 1973.

Shermis, S. Samuel. *Philosophic Foundations of Education.* New York: D. Van Nostrand Company, 1967.

Silberman, Charles E. *Crisis in the Classroom: The Remaking of American Education.* New York: Vintage Books, 1970.

Skinner, B. F. *About Behaviorism.* New York: Vintage Books, 1976.

Skinner, B. F. *Beyond Freedom and Dignity.* New York: Alfred A. Knopf, 1971.

Skinner, B. F. *Science and Human Behavior.* New York: The Macmillan Co., 1953.

Skinner, B. F. *Walden Two.* New York: The Macmillan Co., 1948.

Smith, Philip G. *Philosophy of Education: Introductory Studies.* New York: Harper & Row, 1965.

Snow, C. P. *The Two Cultures and the Scientific Revolution.* New York: Cambridge University Press, 1959.

Soltis, Jonas F. *An Introduction to the Analysis of Educational Concepts.* 2d ed. Reading, Mass.: Addison-Wesley Publishing Co., 1978.

Spencer, Herbert. *Education: Intellectual, Moral, and Physical.* New York: D. Appleton and Co., 1909.

Stretch, Bonnie Barrett. "The Rise of the 'Free School.'" In *Curriculum: Quest for Relevance.* 2d ed. Edited by William Van Til. Boston: Houghton Mifflin Co., 1974.

Task Force in Education for Economic Growth. *Action for Excellence.* Denver: Education Commission of the States, 1983.

Thorndike, Edward L. "The Nature, Purposes, and General Methods of Measurement of Educational Products." In *The Measurement of Educational Products.* National Society for the Study of Education, Seventeenth Yearbook, Part II. Bloomington, Ill.: Public School Publishing Co., 1918.

Titus, Harold, and Smith, Marilyn S. *Living Issues in Philosophy.* 6th ed. New York: D. Van Nostrand Co., 1974.

Toffler, Alvin. *Future Shock.* New York: Random House, 1970.

Toffler, Alvin. *The Third Wave.* New York: Bantam Books, 1980.

Trueblood, David Elton. *General Philosophy.* New York: Harper & Row, 1963.

Trueblood, David Elton. *Philosophy of Religion.* New York: Harper & Row, 1957.

Trueblood, David Elton. *A Place to Stand.* New York: Harper & Row, 1969.

Unamuno, Miguel de. *Tragic Sense of Life.* Translated by J. E. C. Flitch. New York: Dover Publications, 1954.

Van Doren, Mark. *Liberal Education*. Boston: Beacon Press, 1959.

Warnock, Mary. *Ethics Since 1900*, 3d ed. New York: Oxford University Press, 1978.

Wayson, William W. et al. *Up from Excellence: The Impact of the Excellence Movement on Schools*. Bloomington, Indiana: Phi Delta Kappa Educational Foundation, 1988.

Whitehead, Alfred North. *The Aims of Education and Other Essays*. New York: The Free Press, 1967.

Wild, John. *The Challenge of Existentialism*. Bloomington, Indiana: Indiana University Press, 1955.

Wittgenstein, Ludwig. *Tractatus Logico-Philosophicus*. Translated by D. F. Pears and B. F. McGuinness. London: Routledge and Kegan Paul, 1961.

# INDEX

151

153

Synthesis, as a form of philosophical activity, 4
Synthetic statements, 57-58

Teacher (*see also* Educator):
a demonstrator, 52-53;
a facilitator, 80;
a guide, 70-71, 88-89;
a mental disiplinarian, 60;
an example of the Absolute Being,
47;
a spiritual leader, 60;
parent as, 11
Teleology, 15
Television, 11n
Ten Commandments, 69
Theism, 16
Theology, as an aspect of meta-
physics, 15
Thomism, 56, 98
Thorndike, Edward L., 53
Thought, complete act of, 67-68, 70
Titus, Harold H., 29
Toffler, Alvin, 113-14
Training, defined, 9-10
Trueblood, D. Elton, 18, 27n
Truth (*see also* Epistemology and
Knowledge): choice and, 77;

ideas and, 44;
observation and 50;
rationalism and, 57;
what works and, 67

Unamuno, Miguel de, 75
Universal truths, 19, 42
Universe (*see* Cosmos)

Values (*see also* Axiology): from nature, 51;
from society, 68;
from the ideal world, 45;
from the individual, 78;
operative vs. conceived, 28-29;
related to rationality, 58
Vienna Circle, 126-27
Vocational education, 100, 103

Washburne, Carleton, 86
Watson, John B., 116-17
Weingartner, Charles, 1-2
Whitehead, Alfred North, 123, 126
Wild, John, 132
Wilson, Woodrow, 85
Wittgenstein, Ludwig, 125-26, 128